AF364999

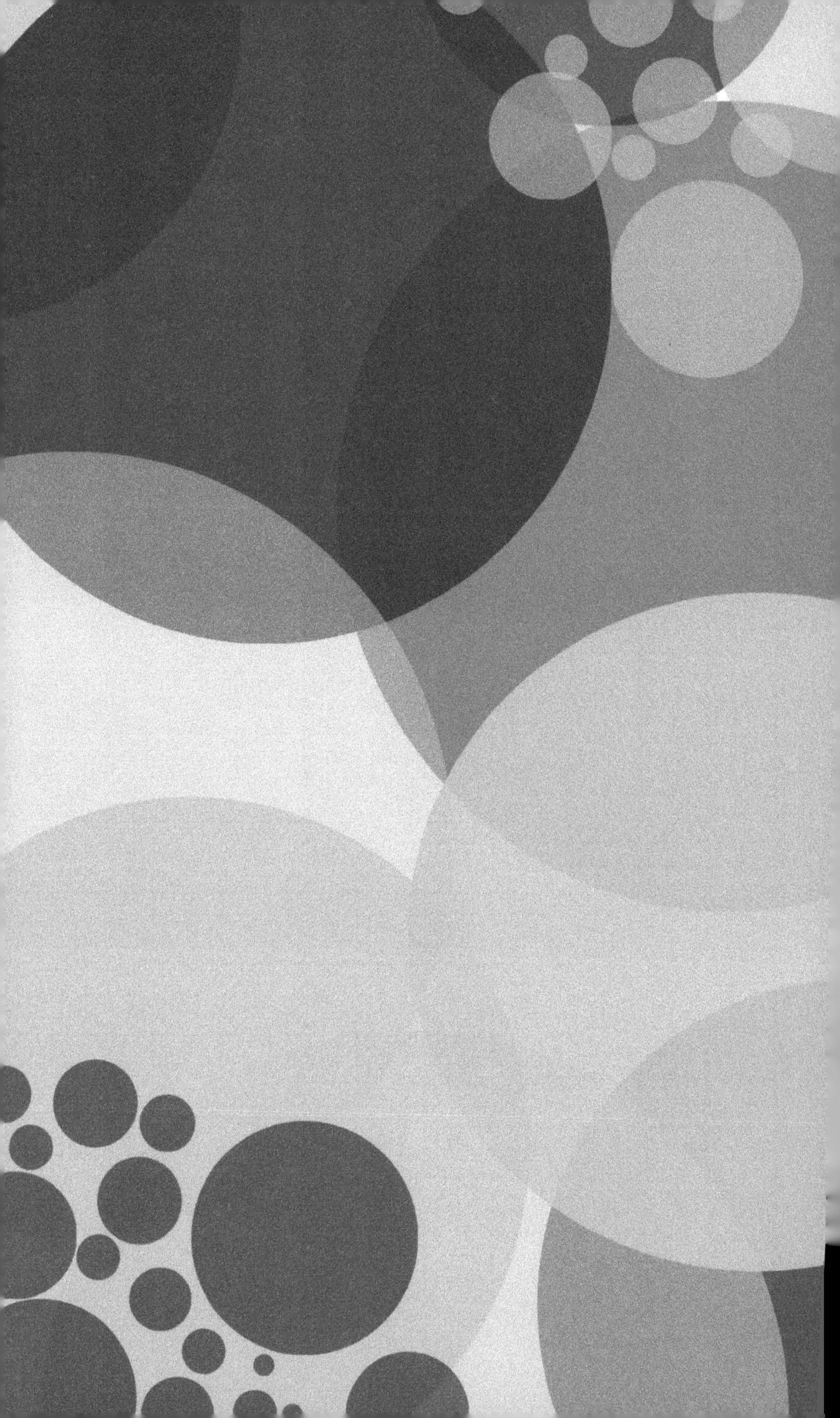

UNVEILING

BUDAPEST

HUNGARY

Your Travel Guide to The Pearl of the Danube

ESSENTIALS EDITION

HUNGARY UNVEILED SERIES

Presented by

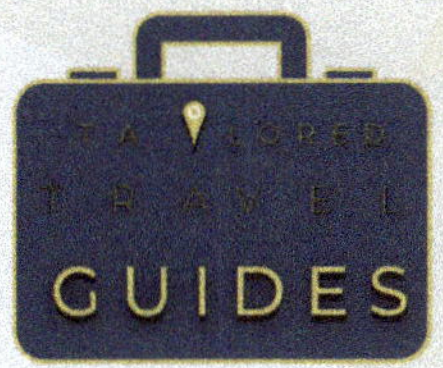

Discover Your Journey

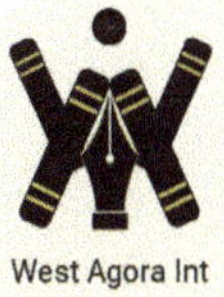

WEST AGORA INT
Timișoara 2024
www.tailoredtravelguides.com
WEST AGORA INT S.R.L. All Rights Reserved

Descrierea CIP a Bibliotecii Nationale a Romaniei
Unveiling Budapest - Hungary: Your Travel Guide to the Pearl of The
Danube. - Essentials Edition. - Timisoara : West Agora
Int, 2024
    ISBN 978-606-95923-7-3
913

W I K I

Budapest: The Pearl of the Danube

Budapest, the capital city of Hungary, is a fascinating metropolis located on the banks of the Danube River in Central Europe. Known as the "Pearl of the Danube," Budapest is not only Hungary's political, cultural, and economic center but also a city rich in history and charm. The city's unique atmosphere is a result of its division into two parts: Buda and Pest, which were unified in 1873, together with Óbuda, creating the modern metropolis known today.

Historically, Budapest's roots can be traced back to Roman times, with the ancient town of Aquincum, which was founded around AD 100 and served as a significant Roman military base and town. The city became a significant economic and political center during the medieval period, especially after the Mongol invasion of Hungary in the 13th century. Budapest played a crucial role during the Ottoman Empire's rule in the 16th and 17th centuries and later during the Austrian Empire, where it became a co-capital of the Austro-Hungarian Empire, contributing significantly to the region's development.

Budapest is renowned for its stunning architecture, from Gothic and Baroque to Art Nouveau, and its extensive World Heritage sites, including the banks of the Danube, the Buda Castle Quarter, and Andrássy Avenue. The city is also famous for its thermal baths, which were used during Roman times and further developed during the Turkish occupation.

Prominent individuals from Budapest include Hungary's famous composers Béla Bartók and Zoltán Kodály, Nobel laureate scientist Albert Szent-Györgyi, and legendary Hollywood film stars like Tony Curtis and Bela Lugosi. These figures highlight the city's diverse contributions

WIKI

to culture, science, and entertainment.

Budapest's identity is deeply entwined with its musical and literary traditions, vibrant arts scene, and the enduring legacy of its spa culture. The city hosts numerous festivals, including the Budapest Spring Festival and Sziget Festival, which draw international crowds and showcase its lively cultural scene.

However, Budapest faces several challenges, including political polarization and issues related to urban development and preservation of its historical sites. The city's inhabitants are also grappling with the impacts of tourism on housing and local infrastructure, alongside broader national concerns like demographic changes and economic disparities.

Controversially, Budapest has been at the forefront of debates over democratic backsliding in Hungary, with tensions between national government policies and the city's more liberal, progressive urban policies. This has been particularly evident in clashes over cultural and educational autonomy, and issues of national versus European identity.

In sum, Budapest is a city of contrasts and confluences, where history and modernity meet against a backdrop of architectural beauty and cultural richness, making it a compelling destination for anyone interested in the layers that make up a dynamic European capital.

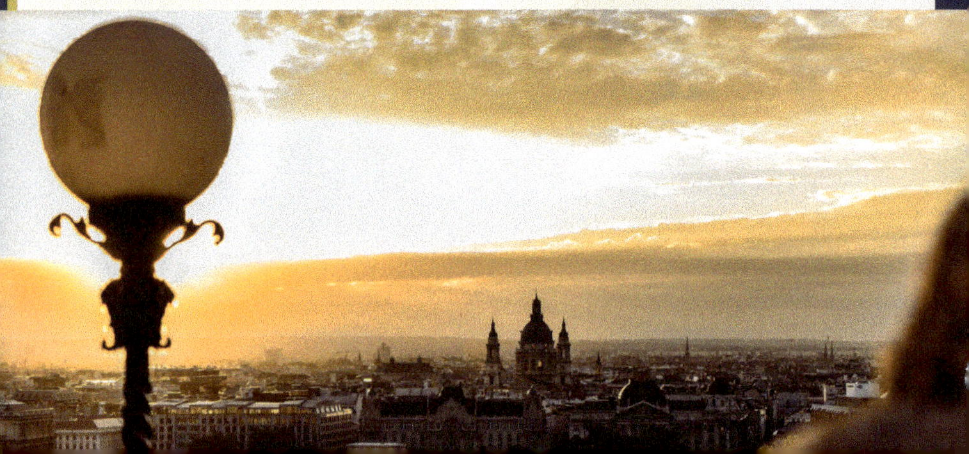

CONTENTS

1 GREETINGS AND RECOMMENDATIONS FROM LOCALS

PRACTICAL INFORMATION 3

10 TOP ATTRACTIONS

HIDDEN GEMS AND LESSER-KNOWN SIGHTS 22

31 PARKS AND GARDENS

CULINARY SCENE 35

40 SHOPPING

FAMILY-FRIENDLY ACTIVITIES 43

46 BUDAPEST BY NIGHT

ART AND CULTURE IN BUDAPEST 58

62 HISTORICAL AND ARCHITECTURAL LANDMARKS

DAY TRIPS FROM BUDAPEST 66

76 END NOTE

BUDAPEST

THE PEARL OF THE DANUBE

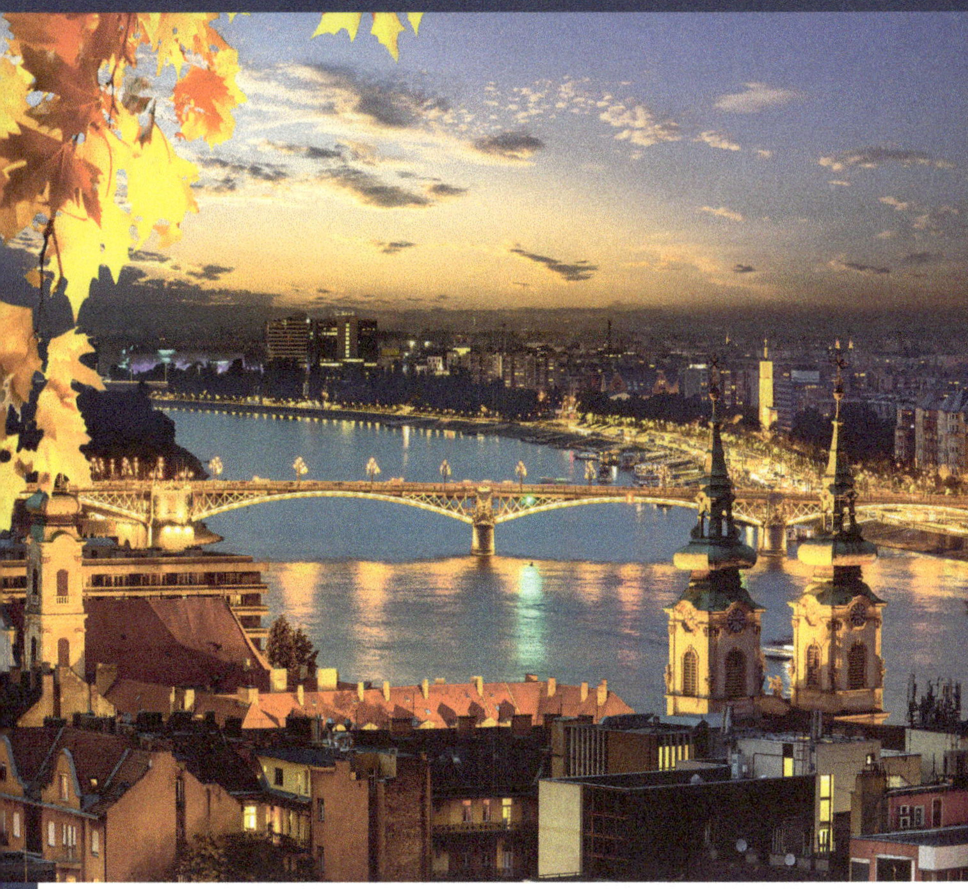

Welcome to Budapest, Hungary's enchanting capital city, where history meets modernity in a spectacular blend of architectural wonders, vibrant cultural scenes, and culinary delights. Nestled along the banks of the majestic Danube River, Budapest is renowned for its stunning landscapes, iconic landmarks, and rich history that spans centuries. From the grandeur of Buda Castle to the picturesque Fisherman's Bastion, the city offers a visual feast that captivates visitors at every turn.

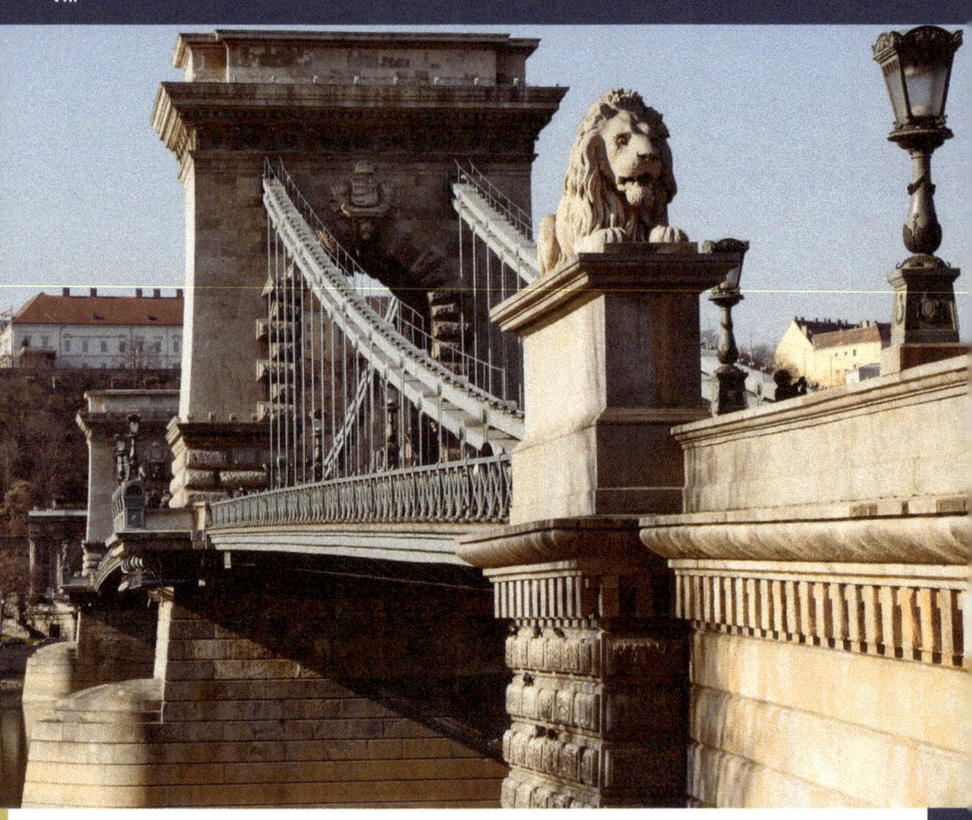

Budapest is often referred to as the "Paris of the East," and for good reason. The city's unique blend of Eastern and Western influences creates a dynamic atmosphere that is both cosmopolitan and deeply rooted in tradition. Whether you're exploring the historic streets of Buda, the bustling boulevards of Pest, or relaxing in one of the city's famed thermal baths, Budapest promises an unforgettable experience filled with discovery and delight.

This travel guide is designed to help you navigate Budapest's myriad attractions, hidden gems, and local secrets. From practical information to detailed descriptions of the city's top sights, you'll find everything you need to make the most of your visit. Whether you're a first-time visitor or a seasoned traveler, our comprehensive guide will ensure you uncover the best of Budapest, from its grand landmarks to its cozy, off-the-beaten-path treasures.

GREETINGS AND INSIGHTS FROM LOCALS

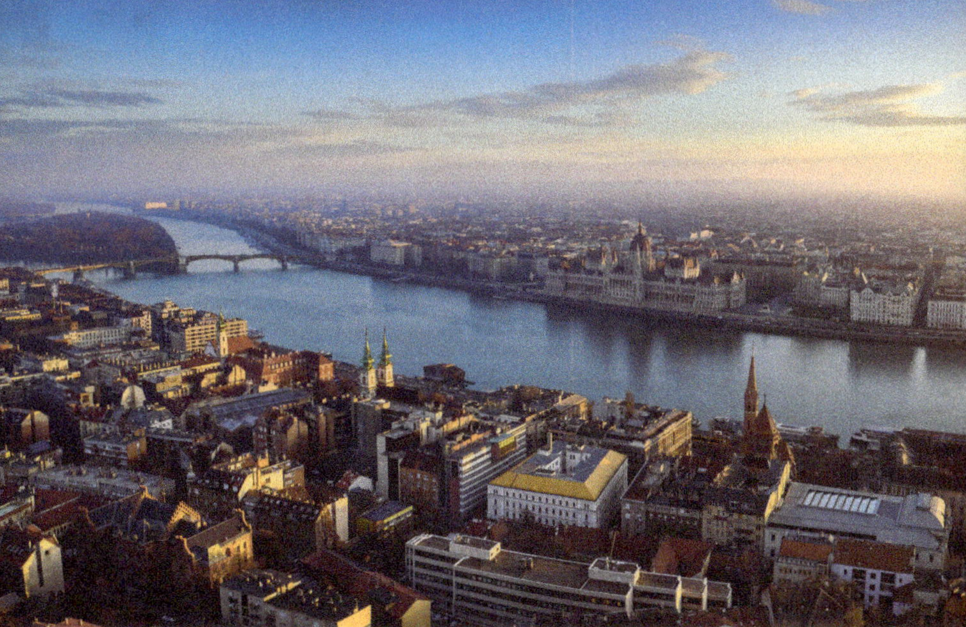

Üdvözöljük, dear traveler! Welcome to Budapest, the Pearl of the Danube, where majestic history flows alongside vibrant modernity in a city that captivates the heart. As a proud Budapester, I've wandered through our city's storied avenues and serene riverbanks, and I'm thrilled to guide you through the hidden wonders and dynamic experiences that only a local would cherish.

Begin your Budapest journey by embracing our warm hospitality. A hearty "szia" and a friendly nod will open doors to a world of discovery in this city of thermal baths and architectural marvels, as you wander from the grandeur of Buda Castle to the lively streets of Pest.

You might find yourself enchanted by the beauty of the Parliament Building, a masterpiece of Gothic Revival architecture. Overlooking the Danube, its intricate facade and majestic interiors tell the story of Hungary's rich political heritage and artistic grandeur.

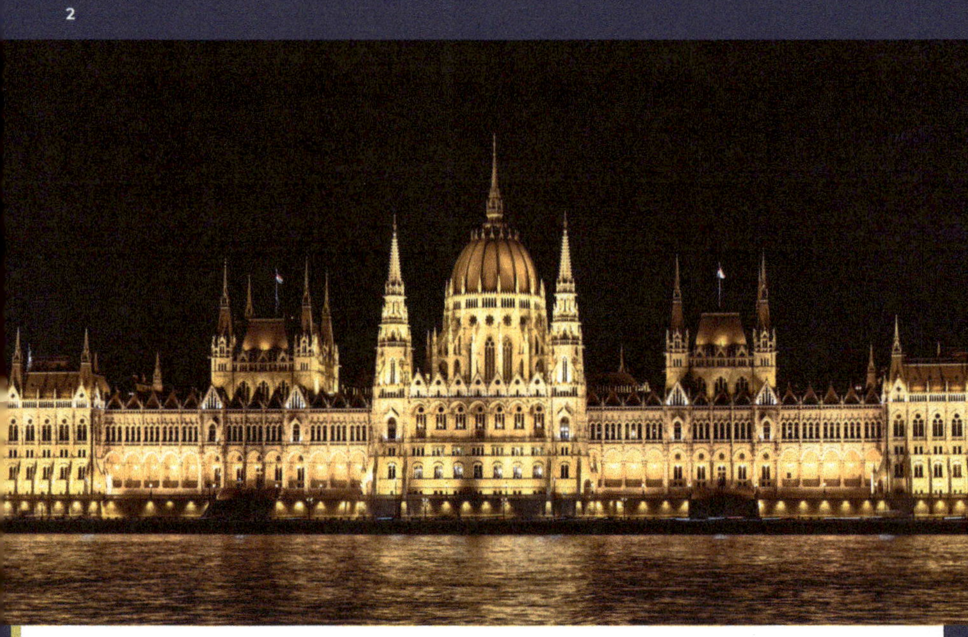

For an immersion in our unique culture, visit the Széchenyi Thermal Bath. This iconic spa, with its grand neo-baroque architecture, offers a rejuvenating experience amidst the city's hustle, evoking Budapest's long-standing tradition of relaxation and wellness.

When the allure of local flavors calls, explore the Great Market Hall. Here, under its grand roof, you can indulge in Hungarian delights – from hearty goulash to sweet kürtőskalács. Each dish here is a celebration of our rich culinary heritage.

As dusk falls, the vibrant energy of the Jewish Quarter beckons. This historic district, with its ruin bars and eclectic eateries, pulses with the city's youthful spirit, offering a perfect backdrop for an evening of exploration and enjoyment.

Nestled along the river, the Shoes on the Danube Bank memorial powerfully commemorates a tragic chapter in Budapest's history, offering a poignant moment of reflection and remembrance.

Budapest's essence lies in its harmonious blend of history, culture, and innovation. We, the Budapesters, are here with open hearts, ready to share the charm and surprises of our beloved city with you. Viszontlátásra, dear traveler, and may your time in Budapest be as enriching and memorable as the stories flowing along the Danube!

PRACTICAL INFORMATION

Currency

Hungary's official currency is the Hungarian Forint (HUF). While some places accept euros, it's best to use forints for all transactions to avoid unfavorable exchange rates. ATMs are widely available, and credit cards are accepted in most establishments.

Transportation

Budapest boasts an efficient and comprehensive public transportation system, including buses, trams, and a metro network. The Budapest Card offers unlimited travel on public transport and discounts at various attractions. Taxis are also available but ensure they are licensed, or use reputable ride-sharing services like Bolt.

Driving in Budapest

Driving in Budapest can be challenging due to narrow streets and heavy traffic. If you choose to drive, be aware that parking in the city center can be scarce and expensive. Consider using public transportation or walking to explore the city's main attractions.

Climate

Budapest experiences a temperate continental climate, with hot summers and cold winters. Spring and autumn are ideal for visiting, offering mild temperatures and fewer tourists. Summers can be humid, while winters often bring snow and frost.

Language

The official language is Hungarian. While many people in the tourism industry speak English, learning a few basic Hungarian phrases can enhance your experience and help you connect with locals.

Power sockets and adapters

Hungary uses Type C and F power sockets with a standard voltage of 230V. If your devices use a different plug type, be sure to bring a suitable adapter.

Shopping

Budapest offers a wide range of shopping experiences, from luxury boutiques on Andrassy Avenue to local markets like the Great Market Hall. Be sure to explore these spots for unique souvenirs and local products.

Tipping

Tipping is customary in Budapest, typically around 10-15% of the bill in restaurants and cafés. It's also common to tip taxi drivers and hotel staff. Ensure to check if a service charge is already included before adding a tip.

USEFUL LINKS AND PHONE NUMBERS

Emergency Services

All Emergencies: 112
Police: 107
Fire Brigade: 105
Medical Emergencies: 104

Transportation

Budapest Liszt Ferenc International **Airport**: +36 1 296 9696, www.bud.hu/en
Budapest **Public Transport** (BKK): +36 1 325 5255, www.bkk.hu/en/
Budapest Keleti **Railway Station**: +36 1 313 6835, www.mavcsoport.hu/en
Főtaxi (Official **Taxi Service**): +36 1 222 2222, www.fotaxi.hu/en/ \

Tourist Information

Budapest **Tourism Office**: +36 1 438 8080, www.budapestinfo.hu/en
Budapest **City Pass**: www.budapestinfo.hu/en/budapest-card
Hungary's **Tourism Office**: www.visithungary.com

Hospitals

Semmelweis University **Hospital**: +36 1 459 1500, www.semmelweis.hu/english/

Local Government

City of Budapest: +36 1 327 1000, www.budapest.hu/en

Maps

For print versions - quick acces through QR codes after the End Note

Budapest maps: www.ontheworldmap.com/hungary/city/budapest/
Budapest General Map: www.ontheworldmap.com/hungary/city/budapest/budapest-street-map.jpg
Budapest City Center Map: www.ontheworldmap.com/hungary/city/budapest/budapest-city-centre-map.jpg
Buda Transport Map: www.ontheworldmap.com/hungary/city/budapest/buda-transport-map.jpg
Pest Transport Map: www.ontheworldmap.com/hungary/city/budapest/central-pest-transport-map.jpg
Budapest Boat Transport Map: www.ontheworldmap.com/hungary/city/budapest/budapest-boat-map.jpg

BUDAPEST AND SURROUNDINGS

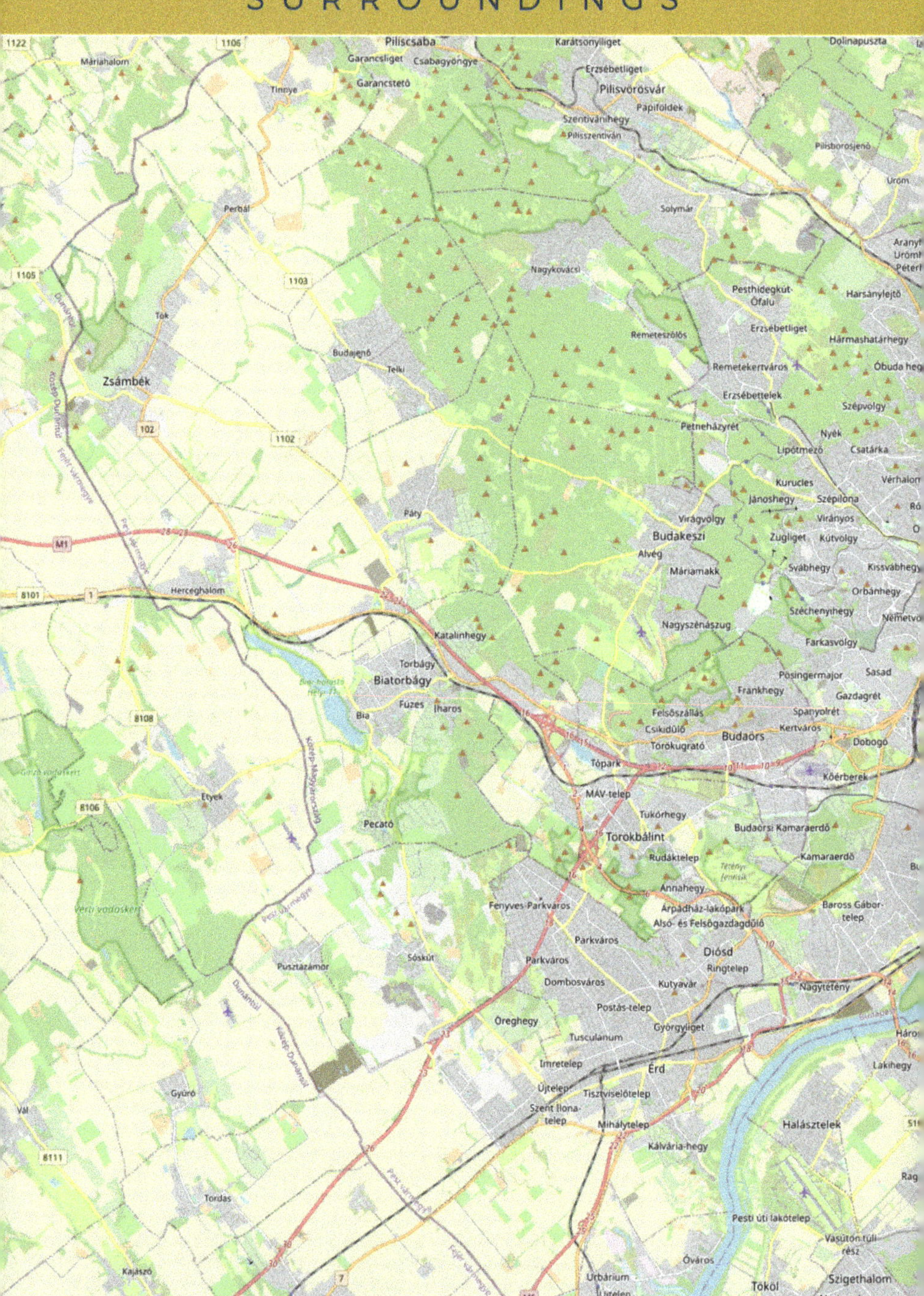

BUDAPEST AND SURROUNDINGS

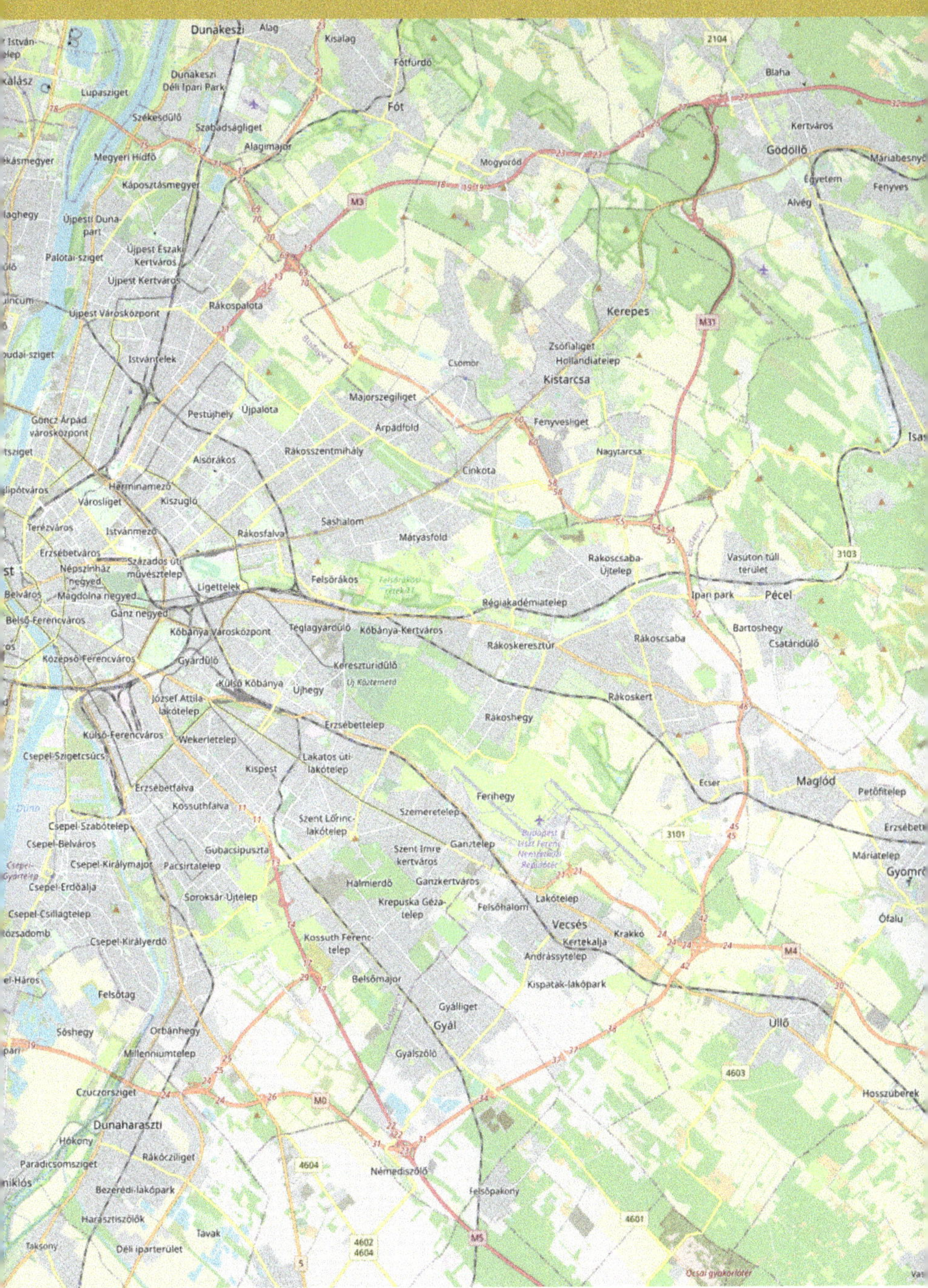

BUDAPEST CITY CENTER MAP

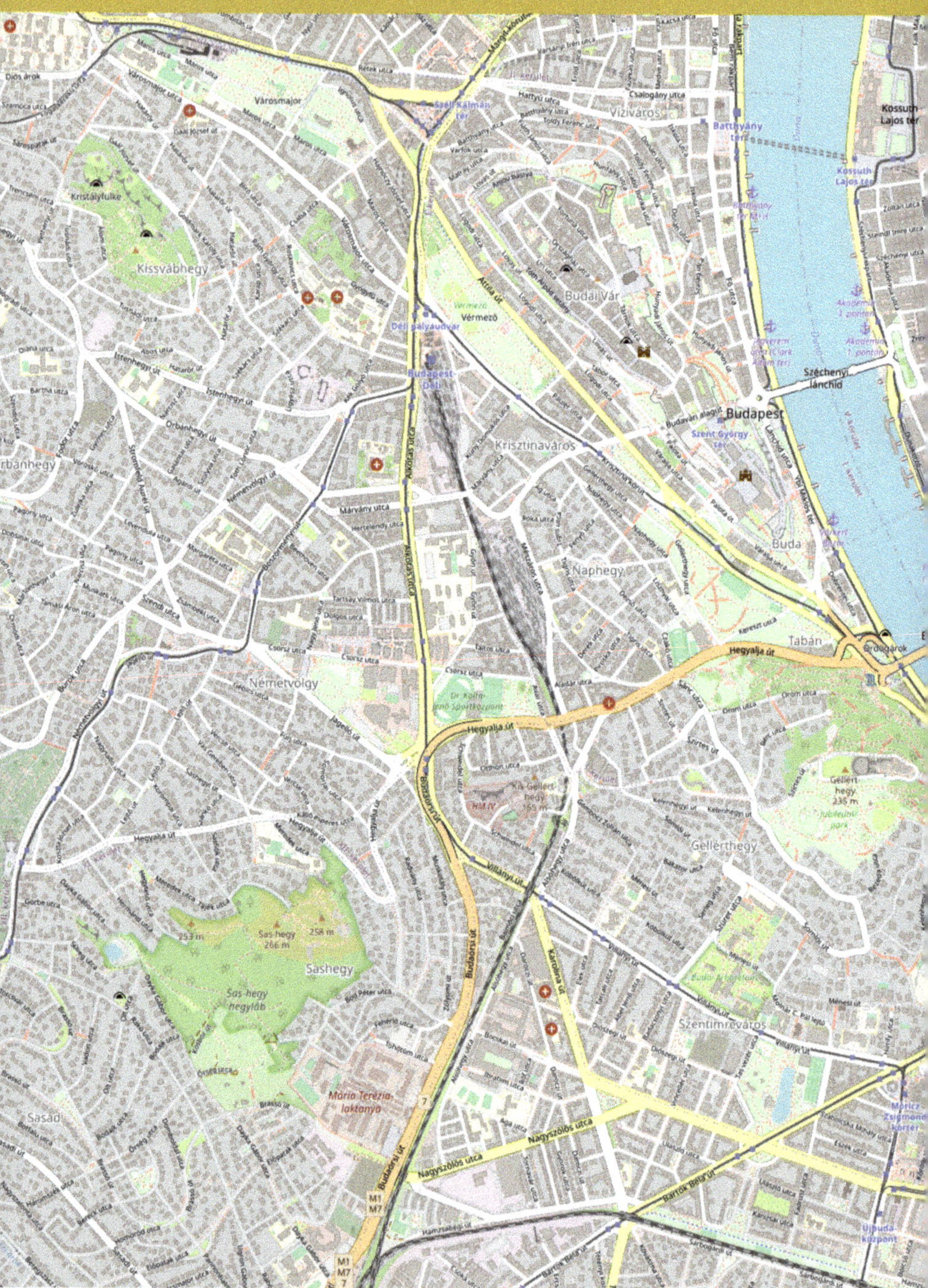

BUDAPEST CITY CENTER MAP

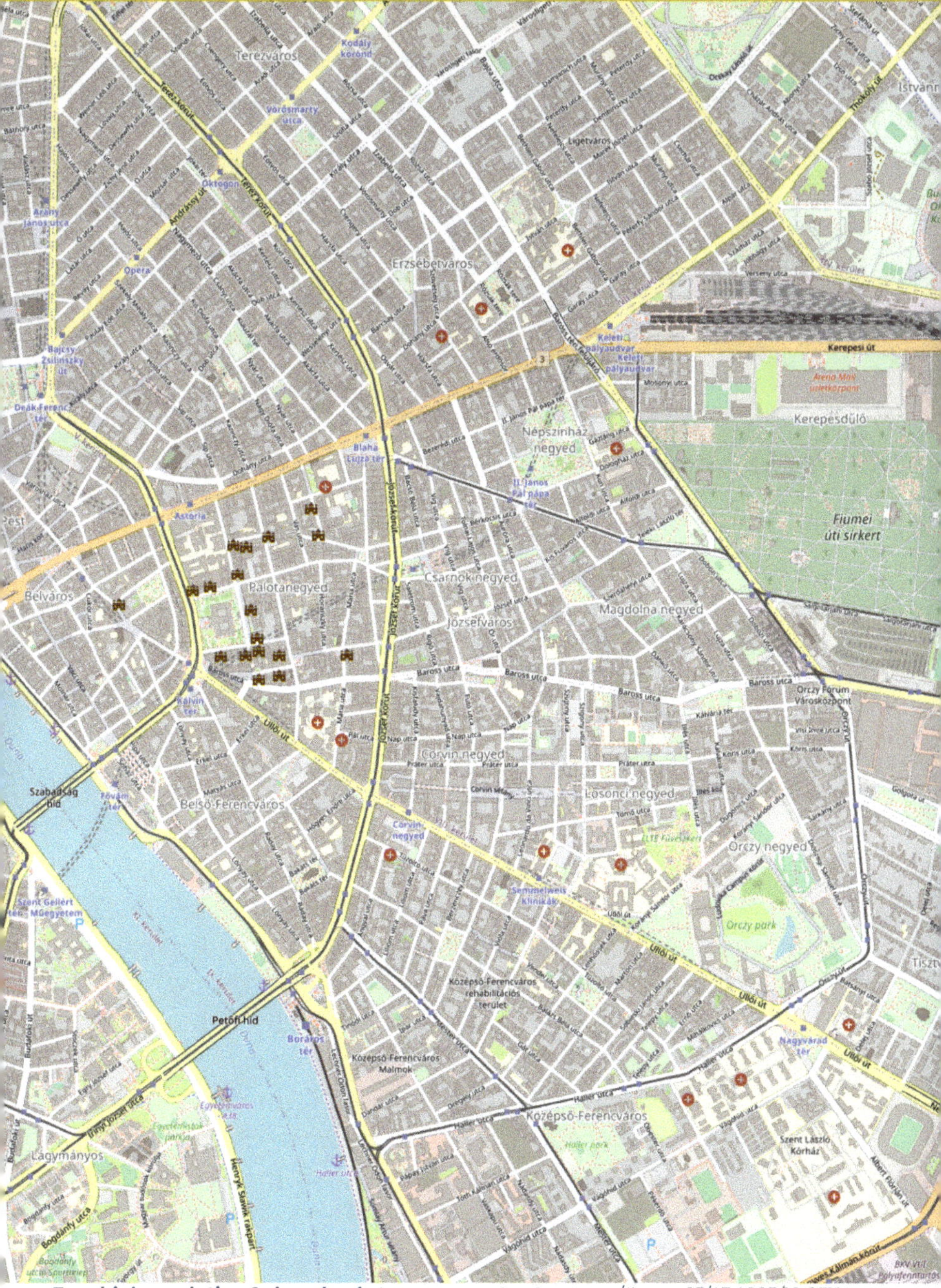

BUDA CASTLE

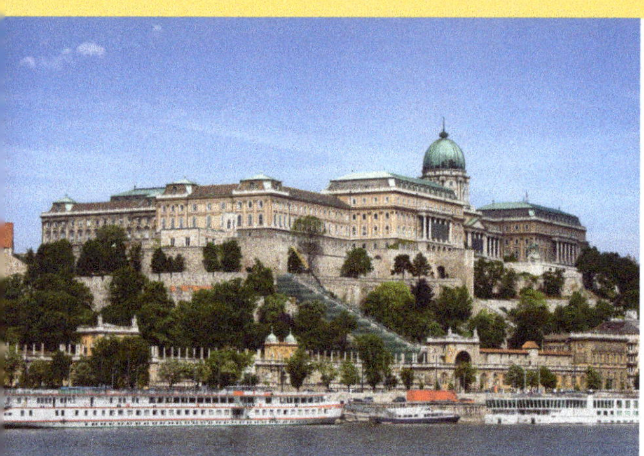

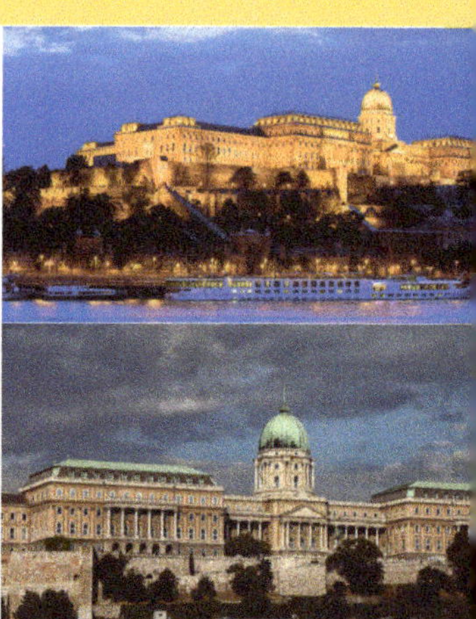

Buda Castle, perched majestically on Castle Hill, is a UNESCO World Heritage Site and a symbol of Hungary's rich history and culture. This impressive Baroque palace complex dates back to the 13th century and has witnessed numerous historical events and transformations. Today, it houses the Hungarian National Gallery and the Budapest History Museum, offering visitors a deep dive into the country's art, history, and cultural heritage. The castle grounds provide stunning panoramic views of the Danube River, the Chain Bridge, and the Pest side of the city.

Exploring Buda Castle, you can wander through its courtyards, admire its architectural splendor, and visit the Matthias Fountain and the Lion Courtyard. The castle often hosts various cultural events, exhibitions, and festivals, making it a vibrant part of Budapest's cultural scene. Don't miss the evening illumination, which casts a magical glow over the entire complex.

Tip: Plan your visit around sunset to enjoy breathtaking views of Budapest as the city lights up. The Fisherman's Bastion and the Chain Bridge look especially enchanting from this vantage point. Also, consider taking the funicular railway from Clark Ádám Square for a scenic and convenient ascent to the castle.

Address: Szent György tér 2, 1014 Budapest, Hungary

Website: www.budacastlebudapest.com

FISHERMAN'S BASTION

Fisherman's Bastion is one of Budapest's most iconic landmarks, offering a fairytale-like experience with its neo-Gothic and neo-Romanesque architecture. Constructed between 1895 and 1902, this magnificent terrace was designed by Frigyes Schulek and provides some of the best panoramic views of Budapest, including the stunning Hungarian Parliament Building and the Danube River. The Bastion's seven towers symbolize the seven Magyar tribes that founded Hungary in the 9th century, adding historical significance to its architectural beauty.

The name "Fisherman's Bastion" is derived from the medieval fishermen's guild that was responsible for defending this part of the city walls. Today, visitors can explore the bastion's terraces, which are open to the public year-round, offering a picturesque setting perfect for photography and relaxation. Adjacent to the bastion is Matthias Church, another architectural marvel worth visiting. Fisherman's Bastion also features a small café where you can enjoy a coffee or snack while taking in the breathtaking views. During the evenings, the illuminated bastion creates a magical ambiance that shouldn't be missed.

Tip: Visit early in the morning or late in the evening to avoid the crowds and enjoy a more serene experience. Consider purchasing a ticket to access the upper terraces for an even more spectacular view. Also, don't forget to visit the nearby Matthias Church for a complete historical experience.

Address: 1-3 Hess Andras Square, Budapest, District I, 1014 Budapest, Hungary

Website: www.fishermansbastion.com

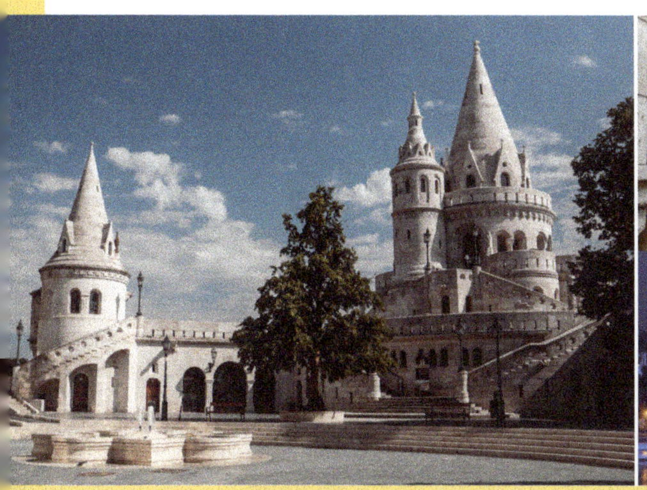

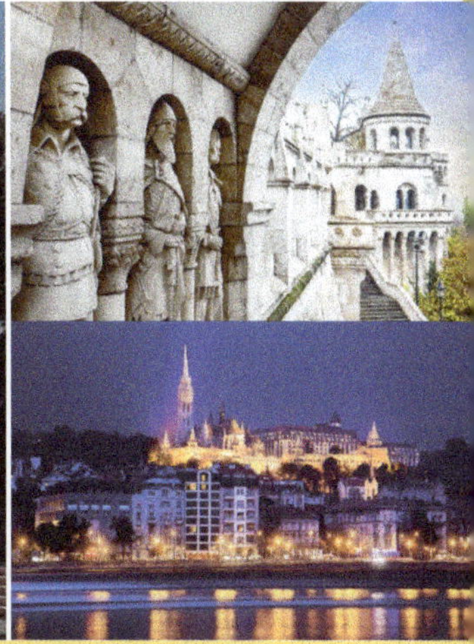

HUNGARIAN PARLIAMENT BUILDING

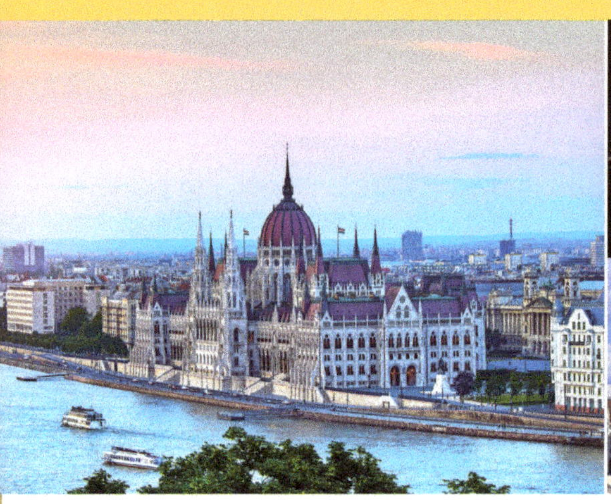

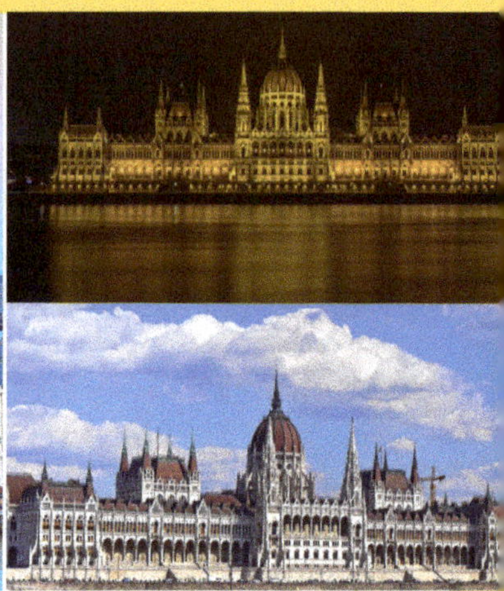

The Hungarian Parliament Building is a magnificent example of Neo-Gothic architecture and one of Budapest's most iconic landmarks. Completed in 1904, this architectural masterpiece is the third largest parliament building in the world and a symbol of Hungary's national identity. Designed by architect Imre Steindl, the building features a stunning façade adorned with intricate carvings, statues, and spires, making it a visual feast for visitors.

Located on the Pest side of the Danube River, the Parliament Building houses the National Assembly of Hungary and is home to several important national treasures, including the Holy Crown of Hungary. Guided tours are available in multiple languages, offering insights into the building's history, architecture, and the country's political system. Inside, you'll find grand staircases, lavish halls, and a central dome that is truly awe-inspiring.

The exterior of the building is equally impressive, particularly when illuminated at night. The reflection of the lit Parliament on the Danube River creates a postcard-perfect scene that is a must-see for any visitor to Budapest.

Tip: Book your tour tickets in advance to secure a spot, as they often sell out quickly. For the best photographs, visit during the golden hour or after sunset when the building is beautifully lit. Don't miss the chance to view it from across the river for a stunning panorama.

Address: Kossuth Lajos tér 1-3, 1055 Budapest, Hungary

Website: www.parlament.hu/en/web/visitors

ST. STEPHEN'S BASILICA

St. Stephen's Basilica is one of Budapest's most revered landmarks and the largest church in Hungary. Named after Stephen I, the first King of Hungary, this neoclassical masterpiece took over 50 years to complete, with construction starting in 1851 and finishing in 1905. The basilica's awe-inspiring architecture features a grand dome, stunning frescoes, and intricate marble work, making it a visual and spiritual centerpiece of the city.

The interior of St. Stephen's Basilica is equally impressive, housing the mummified right hand of St. Stephen, known as the Holy Right Hand, which is a significant relic for Hungarian Catholics. Visitors can explore the richly decorated nave, chapels, and the treasury, which holds numerous religious artifacts. One of the highlights is the panoramic view from the basilica's dome, accessible by an elevator or 364 steps, offering breathtaking vistas of Budapest.St. Stephen's Basilica is not only a place of worship but also a cultural venue, frequently hosting organ concerts and classical music performances that take advantage of its excellent acoustics.

Tip: Visit the basilica during one of its evening concerts for an unforgettable experience. Climb the dome for spectacular views of the city, especially at sunset. Remember to dress modestly, as it is a place of worship, and donations are appreciated for entry.

Address: Szent István tér 1, 1051 Budapest, Hungary
Website: www.bazilika.biz/en

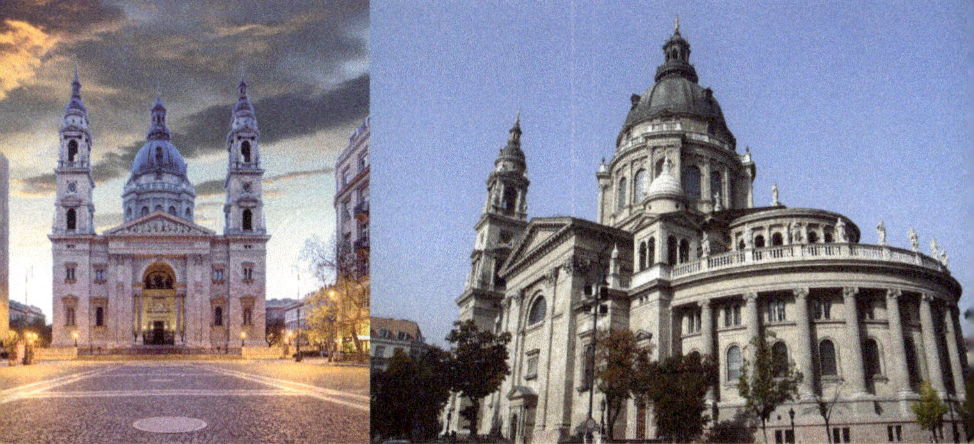

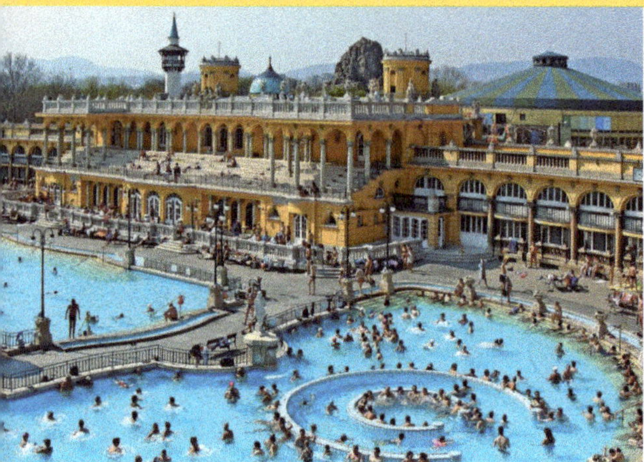
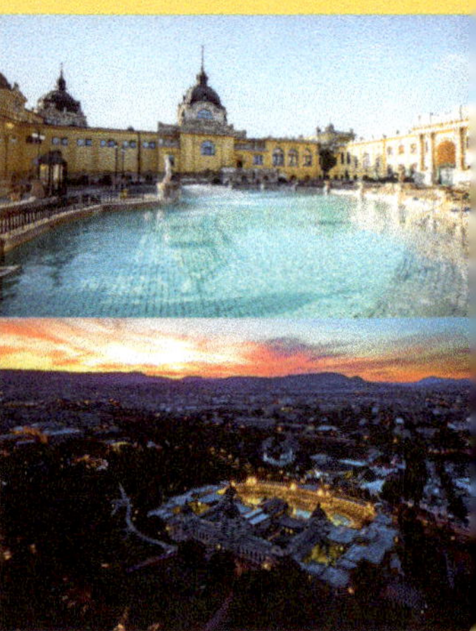

Széchenyi Thermal Bath, located in Budapest's City Park, is one of the largest and most iconic spa complexes in Europe. Opened in 1913, this grandiose neo-baroque building boasts 18 pools, including both indoor and outdoor thermal baths, which are fed by two natural hot springs. The mineral-rich waters are renowned for their therapeutic properties, offering a relaxing and rejuvenating experience.

The outdoor pools, maintained at a comfortable 38°C (100°F) even in winter, are a particular highlight, allowing visitors to soak in the warm waters while enjoying the crisp air and beautiful surroundings. Inside, the complex features various saunas, steam rooms, and treatment areas, providing a comprehensive spa experience. The medicinal waters are rich in calcium, magnesium, and hydrocarbonate, making them beneficial for joint and muscle ailments. Széchenyi Thermal Bath is not just a place for relaxation but also a cultural hub, frequently hosting events such as the popular "Sparty" parties, which combine the spa experience with music and entertainment.

Tip: Arrive early in the morning or late in the evening to avoid crowds and enjoy a more peaceful experience. Bring your own towel and flip-flops to save on rental costs, and consider booking a massage or spa treatment in advance for added relaxation.

Address: Állatkerti krt. 9-11, 1146 Budapest, Hungary
Website: www.szechenyibath.hu

Heroes' Square, or Hősök tere, is one of Budapest's most significant and grandiose landmarks, marking the entrance to City Park. Completed in 1896 to commemorate the 1,000th anniversary of the Magyar conquest of Hungary, this monumental square is dominated by the Millennium Monument, a 36-meter-high column topped with a statue of the Archangel Gabriel holding the Hungarian Holy Crown and apostolic cross.

The square is flanked by two majestic museums: the Museum of Fine Arts on the left and the Hall of Art on the right, both of which are architectural masterpieces housing impressive art collections. At the base of the Millennium Monument, you'll find statues of the seven chieftains who led the Hungarian tribes into the Carpathian Basin, as well as other important national leaders and historical figures.

Heroes' Square is not only a historical site but also a vibrant public space that often hosts national events, celebrations, and public gatherings. Its sheer size and grandeur make it a favorite spot for tourists and locals alike.

Tip: Visit Heroes' Square early in the morning or late in the afternoon to avoid the busiest times and get the best photos. Combine your visit with a trip to the nearby Széchenyi Thermal Bath and the Museum of Fine Arts to make the most of your time in this culturally rich area.

Address: Hősök tere, 1146 Budapest, Hungary
Website: www.budapestinfo.hu/en/heroes-square

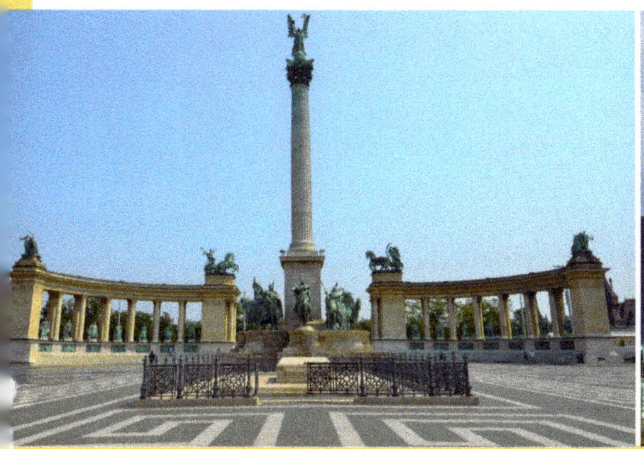

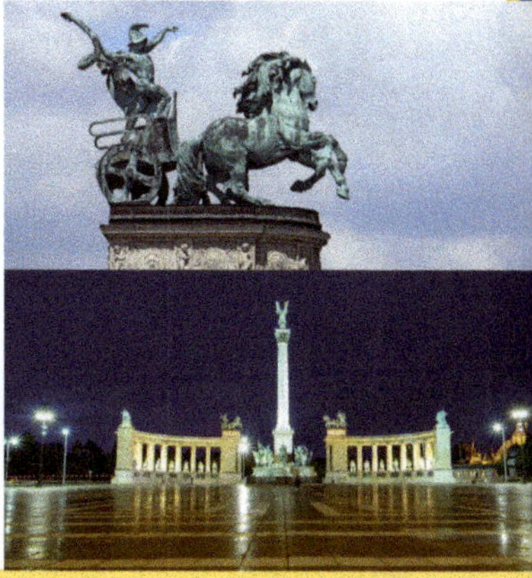

CHAIN BRIDGE

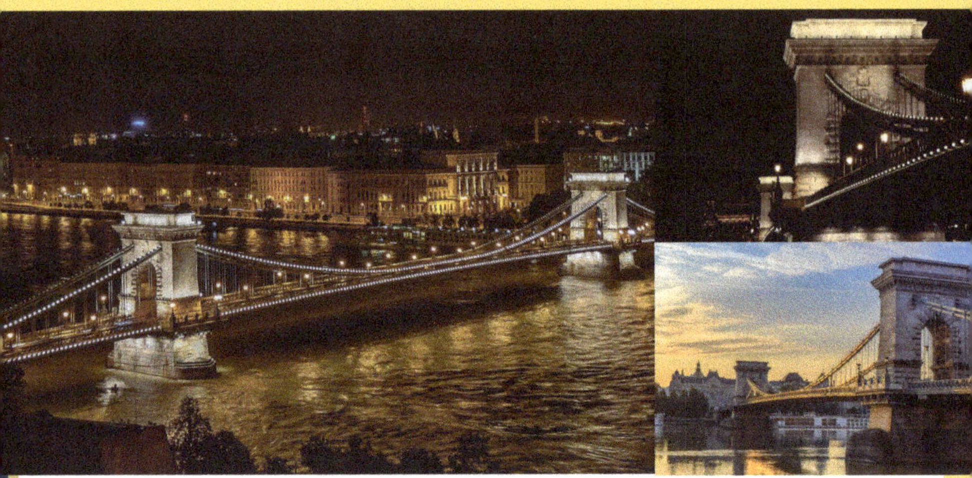

The Széchenyi Chain Bridge, commonly known as the Chain Bridge, is one of Budapest's most iconic landmarks and a symbol of the city's unity. Completed in 1849, it was the first permanent bridge to span the Danube River, connecting the historic Buda and Pest sides of the city. Designed by English engineer William Tierney Clark and supervised by Scottish engineer Adam Clark, the bridge is an architectural marvel of its time, featuring large stone lions at each end and stunning ironwork.

The Chain Bridge offers picturesque views of the city's skyline, including Buda Castle, the Hungarian Parliament Building, and the Fisherman's Bastion. It is especially enchanting at night when it is beautifully illuminated, creating a romantic ambiance perfect for an evening stroll.

Walking across the bridge provides a unique perspective of Budapest and is a must-do activity for visitors. The bridge also plays a significant role in the city's history and culture, having survived wars and reconstructions to remain a vital connection between Buda and Pest.

Tip: Visit the bridge at sunset for breathtaking views and fewer crowds. After crossing, take a leisurely walk along the Danube Promenade or head up to Buda Castle for more stunning vistas. For a unique experience, consider a nighttime river cruise to see the bridge and the city's landmarks beautifully lit.

Address: Széchenyi Lánchíd, 1051 Budapest, Hungary
Website: www.budapestinfo.hu/en/chain-bridge

MATTHIAS CHURCH

Matthias Church, officially known as the Church of Our Lady, is a stunning Gothic structure located in the heart of the Buda Castle District. With its colorful, diamond-patterned roof tiles and ornate spires, the church is one of Budapest's most recognizable landmarks. Established in the 13th century, the church has undergone various renovations and expansions over the centuries, with the current Neo-Gothic design completed in the late 19th century under the direction of architect Frigyes Schulek.

The church's interior is just as impressive as its exterior, featuring intricate frescoes, stained glass windows, and a rich collection of ecclesiastical art. Matthias Church has played a pivotal role in Hungary's history, serving as the coronation site for several Hungarian kings, including the crowning of Franz Joseph I and Charles IV.

Visitors can explore the church's beautiful chapels, the main nave, and the crypt. Additionally, the church often hosts classical music concerts, taking advantage of its excellent acoustics and providing a unique cultural experience.

Tip: Purchase a combined ticket that includes access to the Fisherman's Bastion for an enhanced visit. Don't miss the panoramic views from the Fisherman's Bastion terrace, and try to attend a concert inside the church for an unforgettable experience. Remember to dress modestly, as it is an active place of worship.

Address: Szentháromság tér 2, 1014 Budapest, Hungary
Website: www.matyas-templom.hu/en/

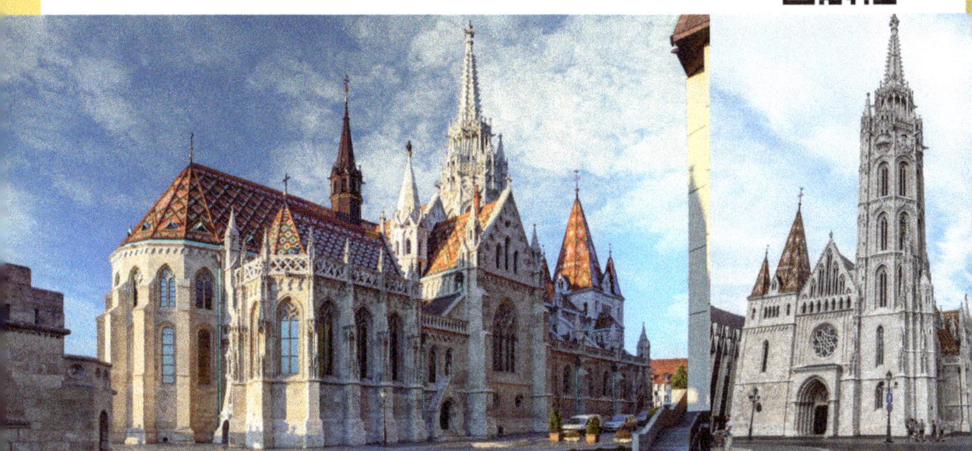

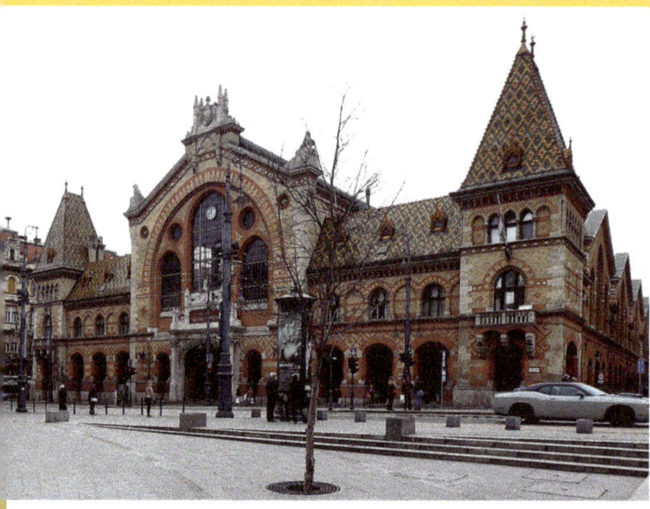

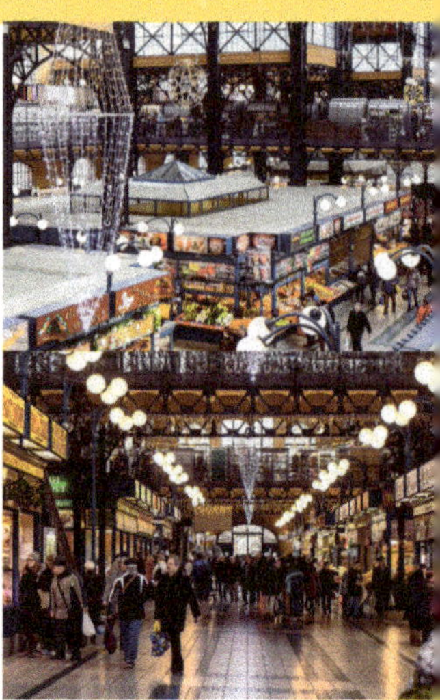

The Great Market Hall, also known as Central Market Hall, is Budapest's largest and oldest indoor market, offering a vibrant and authentic Hungarian shopping experience. Opened in 1897, this impressive neo-Gothic building is located at the end of the famous Váci Street and spans three floors filled with a diverse array of goods. The market's stunning architecture features a distinctive roof adorned with colorful Zsolnay tiles, making it a landmark in its own right.

Inside, the ground floor is bustling with stalls selling fresh produce, meats, cheeses, pastries, and spices, including the famous Hungarian paprika. The upper floor houses a variety of souvenir shops and food vendors, where you can sample traditional Hungarian dishes such as lángos (deep-fried dough with various toppings), goulash, and strudels. The basement level offers fishmongers, pickles, and a supermarket.

The Great Market Hall is not just a shopping destination but also a cultural experience, providing insight into Hungarian culinary traditions and daily life. It's a must-visit for anyone wanting to immerse themselves in the local culture and taste the flavors of Hungary.

Tip: Visit early in the morning to avoid crowds and have the best selection of fresh produce. Don't miss trying lángos from the food stalls on the upper floor—it's a local favorite. Bring cash, as some

vendors may not accept credit cards.

Address: Vámház krt. 1-3, 1093 Budapest, Hungary

Website: www.piaconline.hu/en/central-market-hall/

HUNGARIAN STATE OPERA HOUSE

The Hungarian State Opera House is a breathtaking example of Neo-Renaissance architecture and one of Budapest's most prestigious cultural landmarks. Opened in 1884, the building was designed by renowned Hungarian architect Miklós Ybl. Its opulent interiors feature marble columns, gilded ceilings, and lavish frescoes by some of the most famous artists of the time, making it a true architectural masterpiece.

The Opera House is renowned for its excellent acoustics and has hosted countless world-class opera and ballet performances. The main auditorium seats over 1,200 guests and is adorned with a magnificent chandelier and intricate decorations that create a majestic ambiance. The grand staircase, often considered one of the most beautiful in Europe, adds to the building's splendor.

In addition to performances, the Hungarian State Opera House offers guided tours in multiple languages, providing a fascinating glimpse into its history, architecture, and behind-the-scenes operations. Visitors can explore the elegant foyer, the royal box, and other parts of this historic venue.

Tip: Book tickets for a performance well in advance, as they tend to sell out quickly. If you're unable to attend a performance, the guided tours are an excellent alternative to experience the beauty and history of the Opera House. Don't forget to visit the Opera Café for a delightful experience before or after your tour.

Address: Andrássy út 22, 1061 Budapest, Hungary
Website: www.opera.hu/en/

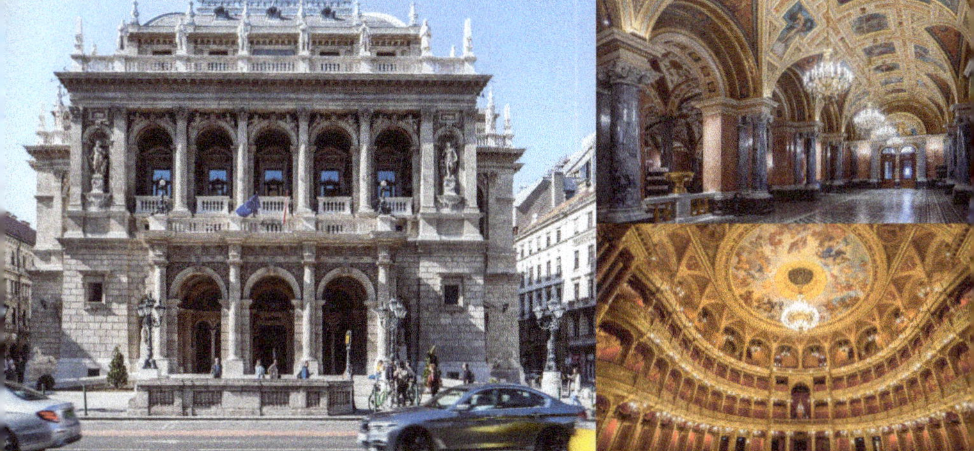

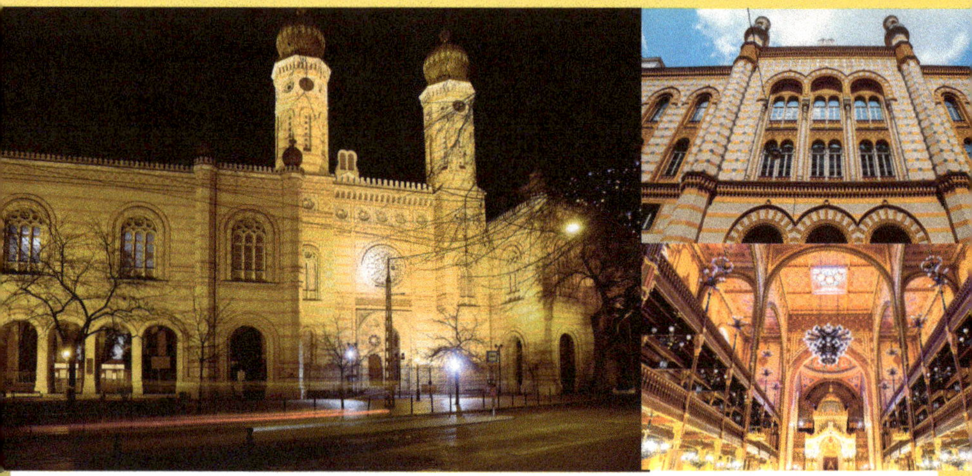

The Dohány Street Synagogue, also known as the Great Synagogue, is the largest synagogue in Europe and the second largest in the world. Located in the heart of Budapest's Jewish Quarter, this stunning building is a masterpiece of Moorish Revival architecture, featuring intricate designs, domes, and stained glass windows. Completed in 1859, it stands as a symbol of the rich Jewish heritage and history in Hungary.

The synagogue complex includes several significant sites. The Hungarian Jewish Museum, located within the synagogue, houses a vast collection of Jewish artifacts and exhibits that narrate the history and culture of Hungarian Jewry. Adjacent to the synagogue is the Holocaust Memorial, also known as the Emanuel Tree, a poignant sculpture resembling a weeping willow tree, with each leaf inscribed with the name of a Holocaust victim. Visitors can explore the beautiful interior of the synagogue, with its ornate decorations, impressive organ, and vast sanctuary that can accommodate 3,000 people. Guided tours are available in multiple languages, offering in-depth insights into the synagogue's history and the Jewish community in Budapest.

Tip: Dress modestly when visiting the synagogue, as it is an active place of worship. Consider joining a guided tour for a more comprehensive understanding of the site's historical significance. Don't miss the nearby Raoul Wallenberg Memorial Park, which is also part of the complex.

Address: Dohány u. 2, 1074 Budapest, Hungary
Website: www.jewishtourhungary.com/en

GELLÉRT HILL AND STATUE

Gellért Hill, rising 235 meters above the Danube River, offers some of the most spectacular panoramic views of Budapest. This prominent hill is named after Saint Gerard (Gellért), who was martyred here in the 11th century. At the hill's peak stands the Liberty Statue, a monumental 14-meter-tall statue of a woman holding a palm leaf, erected in 1947 to commemorate the Soviet liberation of Hungary during World War II.

Gellért Hill is not only a viewpoint but also a site of historical and cultural significance. The Citadella, a fortress built by the Habsburgs in 1854, dominates the hill and provides a glimpse into Budapest's military history. The hill is also home to the Gellért Hill Cave, which houses a chapel and a monastery.

Visitors can enjoy a leisurely hike up the hill, passing through lush greenery and numerous trails. Along the way, several viewpoints offer stunning vistas of the city, the Danube River, and Budapest's famous landmarks like the Parliament Building and Buda Castle. The walk is particularly rewarding at sunset when the city is bathed in golden light.

Tip: Wear comfortable shoes for the hike, and bring a camera to capture the breathtaking views. Consider visiting in the early morning or late afternoon to avoid the midday heat and crowds. The nearby Gellért Thermal Bath is an excellent place to relax after your climb.

Address: Gellérthegy, Budapest, Hungary
Website: www.budapestinfo.hu/en/gellert-hill-and-the-citadel

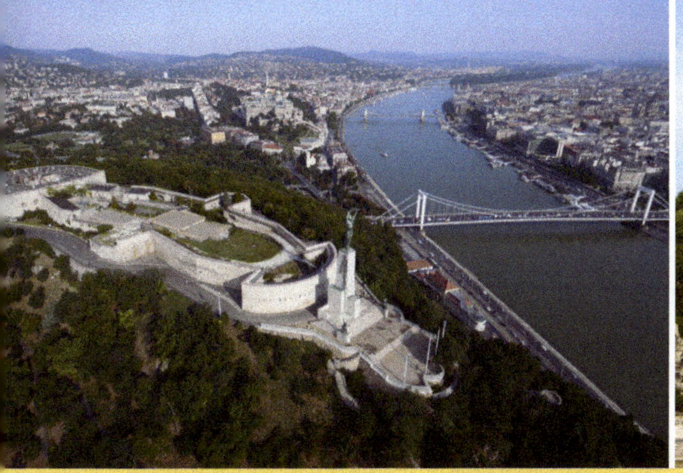

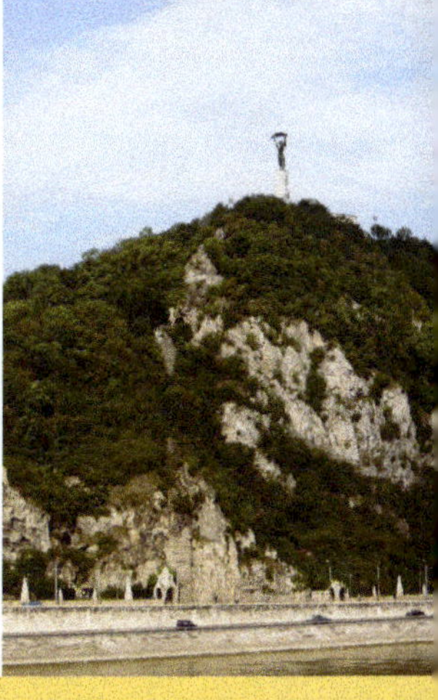

HIDDEN GEMS AND LESSER-KNOWN SIGHTS

SHOES ON THE DANUBE BANK

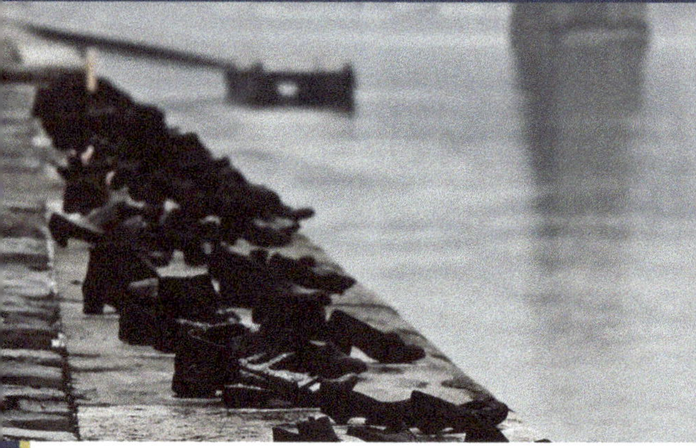

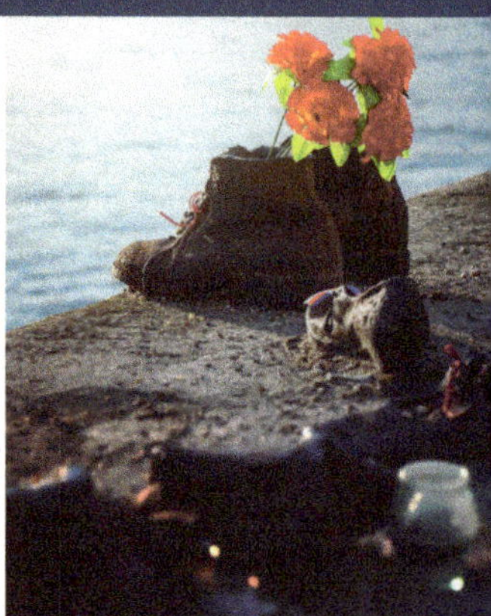

Shoes on the Danube Bank is a poignant memorial located on the Pest side of the Danube River, near the Hungarian Parliament Building. Created in 2005 by sculptor Gyula Pauer and filmmaker Can Togay, this powerful installation commemorates the Jewish victims who were executed by the Arrow Cross militiamen during World War II. The victims were ordered to remove their shoes before being shot at the edge of the river, their bodies falling into the Danube.

The memorial consists of 60 pairs of iron shoes, styled after 1940s footwear, set into the concrete embankment. The shoes vary in style and size, representing the men, women, and children who lost their lives. The simplicity and starkness of the memorial create a powerful and moving tribute to the victims, serving as a reminder of the atrocities committed during the Holocaust.

Visitors to the site often leave candles, flowers, and other mementos in the shoes, adding a personal and emotional touch to the memorial.

Tip: Visit the memorial in the early morning or late afternoon for a quieter and more reflective experience. Take a moment to read the plaques and learn about the history behind the memorial. Consider combining your visit with a walk along the Danube Promenade for a deeper appreciation of Budapest's history and beauty.

Address: Id. Antall József rkp., 1054 Budapest, Hungary
Website: www.budapestinfo.hu/en/shoes-on-the-danube-bank

HOSPITAL IN THE ROCK NUCLEAR BUNKER MUSEUM

The Hospital in the Rock Nuclear Bunker Museum is one of Budapest's most intriguing and lesser-known attractions, offering a fascinating glimpse into the city's wartime history. Located beneath the Buda Castle in a series of natural caves and tunnels, this underground facility served as a secret emergency hospital during World War II and the 1956 Hungarian Revolution. Later, during the Cold War, it was fortified as a nuclear bunker.

The museum features a well-preserved collection of medical equipment, documents, and wax figures that recreate the harrowing conditions and heroic efforts of the doctors and nurses who worked here. Visitors can explore the various rooms and corridors, including the operating theaters, wards, and the command center, all meticulously restored to their original state.

Guided tours, available in multiple languages, provide an in-depth narrative of the hospital's history and its role during significant historical events. The museum also sheds light on the Cold War era, with exhibits on civil defense and the impact of nuclear threats.

Tip: The museum's temperature is kept cool due to its underground location, so bring a light jacket. Booking a guided tour in advance is recommended, as they can fill up quickly. Combine your visit with a trip to the nearby Buda Castle for a full day of historical exploration.

Address: Lovas út 4/c, 1012 Budapest, Hungary
Website: www.sziklakorhaz.eu/en

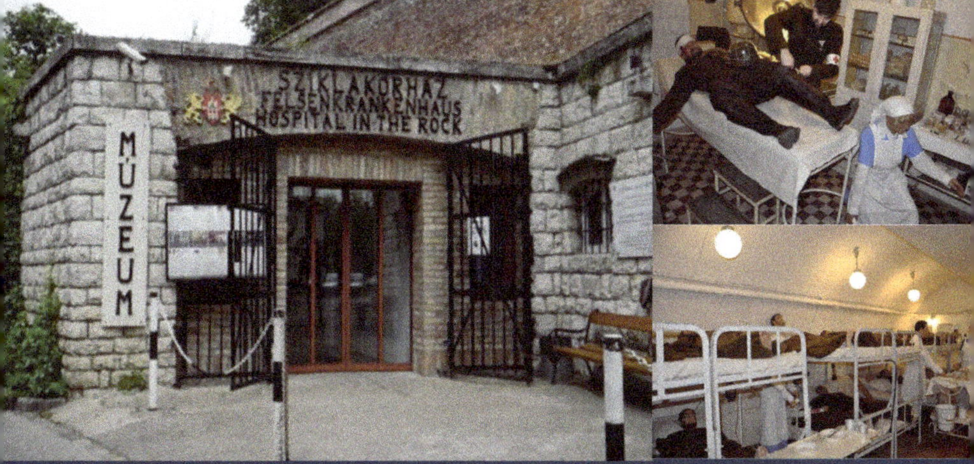

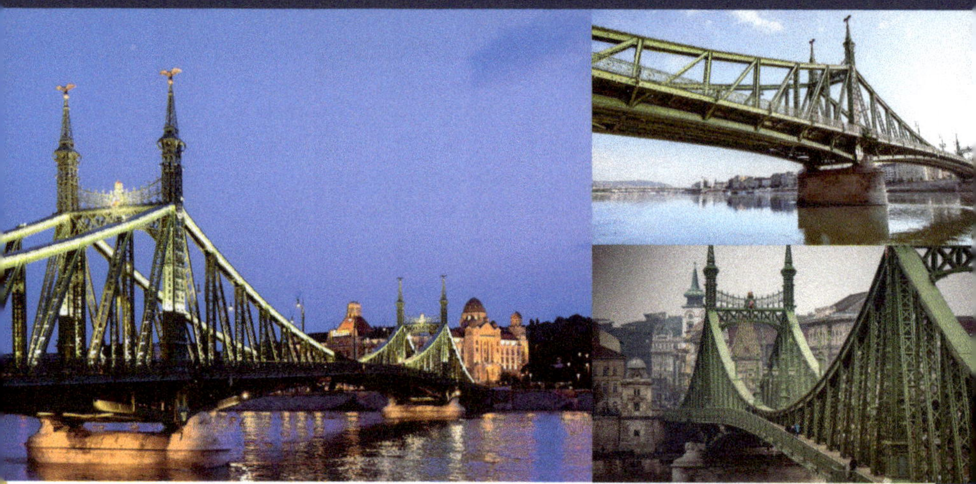

Liberty Bridge, or Szabadság híd, is one of Budapest's most charming and lesser-known landmarks. Completed in 1896 for the Millennium World Exhibition, this picturesque bridge spans the Danube River, connecting the Buda and Pest sides of the city between Gellért Hill and the Great Market Hall. Its striking green iron structure and ornate design, featuring turul bird statues on top of its pillars, make it a standout piece of architecture.

The bridge was originally named Franz Joseph Bridge, after the Habsburg emperor, but was renamed Liberty Bridge after World War II. Despite being destroyed during the war, it was one of the first structures to be rebuilt, symbolizing the resilience and rebirth of the city.

Liberty Bridge is less crowded than other bridges in Budapest, offering a more tranquil walking experience with stunning views of the Danube, Gellért Hill, and the cityscape. It's a favorite spot for both locals and tourists to take leisurely strolls, particularly during sunrise or sunset when the views are exceptionally beautiful.

Tip: Visit early in the morning for a peaceful walk and to capture the best photos without crowds. On weekends, the bridge is often closed to traffic, turning it into a pedestrian-only zone, perfect for a relaxed stroll. Combine your visit with nearby attractions like the Great Market Hall and Gellért Baths for a full day of exploration.

Address: Liberty Bridge, Budapest, Hungary
Website:
www.bridgesofbudapest.com/bridge/liberty_bridge

The Aquincum Museum, located in the Óbuda district of Budapest, offers a fascinating journey back to the Roman era. This open-air museum is built around the ruins of the ancient Roman city of Aquincum, which served as a significant military and administrative center in the province of Pannonia from the 1st to the 4th century AD. The site features well-preserved remnants of Roman baths, homes, marketplaces, and an amphitheater, providing a vivid glimpse into daily life during the Roman Empire.

The museum's indoor exhibits showcase a vast collection of artifacts excavated from the site, including mosaics, statues, inscriptions, and everyday items that highlight the cultural and social aspects of Roman life. Interactive displays and reconstructions help bring history to life, making it an engaging experience for visitors of all ages.

One of the museum's highlights is the reconstructed Roman water organ, which demonstrates the advanced engineering skills of the time. Seasonal events, such as Roman festivals and reenactments, add an extra layer of excitement to your visit.

Tip: Wear comfortable shoes, as there is plenty of walking involved while exploring the extensive outdoor ruins. Plan your visit during the warmer months to fully enjoy the open-air sections of the museum. Consider joining a guided tour for deeper insights into the history and significance of Aquincum. Don't forget to check the museum's calendar for any special events or reenactments during your visit.

Address: Szentendrei út 135, 1031 Budapest, Hungary
Website: www.aquincum.hu/en/

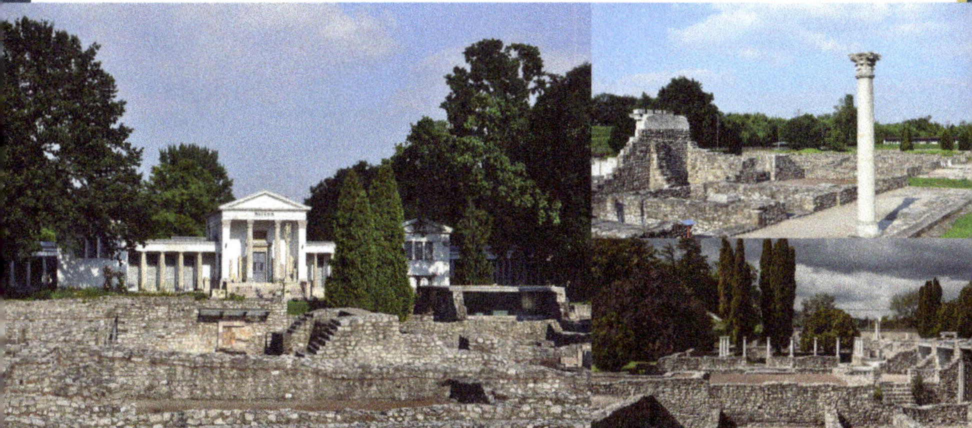

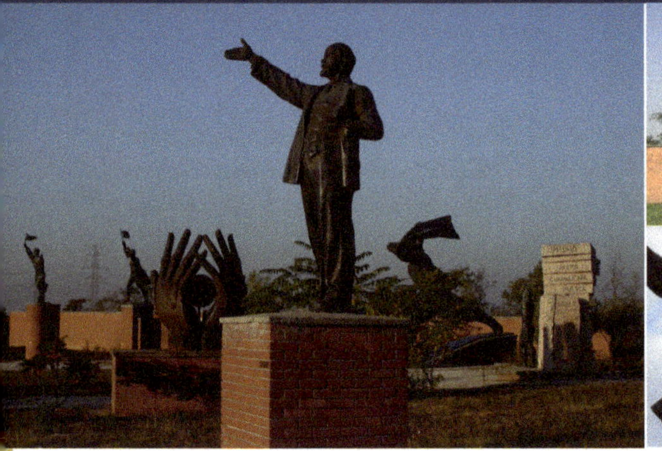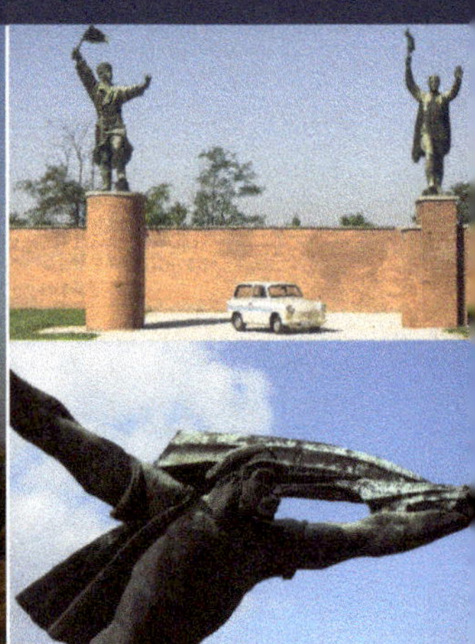

Memento Park, located on the outskirts of Budapest, is an open-air museum dedicated to preserving Hungary's Communist past. This unique park showcases a collection of statues and monuments from the Communist era, which were removed from the streets of Budapest after the fall of the regime in 1989. The park serves as a powerful reminder of Hungary's turbulent history and offers a thought-provoking experience for visitors.

The park is divided into two sections: Statue Park and Witness Square. Statue Park features larger-than-life statues of prominent Communist leaders like Lenin, Marx, and Engels, as well as Hungarian Communist figures. The imposing sculptures are displayed in a way that highlights their original grandeur while also encouraging reflection on the era they represent.

Witness Square includes the grandstand and the exhibition hall, where visitors can watch a documentary on the secret police and view other exhibits related to the Communist regime. The park also houses the "Stalin's Boots" monument, a replica of the boots left behind after the toppling of Stalin's statue in 1956.

Tip: Consider taking the direct bus from Deák Ferenc Square for easy access to the park. Visit the park's small gift shop for unique souvenirs related to Hungary's Communist history. Plan your visit in the morning or late afternoon to avoid the midday heat and enjoy a quieter experience.

Address: Balatoni út – Szabadkai utca sarok, 1223 Budapest, Hungary
Website: www.mementopark.hu/en/home/

CASTLE GARDEN BAZAAR

The Castle Garden Bazaar, or Várkert Bazár, is a hidden gem nestled at the foot of Buda Castle, offering a blend of history, culture, and natural beauty. Originally built between 1875 and 1883, this neo-Renaissance complex was designed by architect Miklós Ybl. After falling into disrepair during the 20th century, the Bazaar underwent extensive restoration and reopened in 2014, reclaiming its place as a cultural hub in Budapest.

The Castle Garden Bazaar features beautifully restored buildings, pavilions, and gardens, providing a picturesque setting for leisurely strolls. The area hosts a variety of cultural events, including concerts, exhibitions, and theater performances, making it a vibrant part of Budapest's cultural scene. The terraces offer stunning views of the Danube River and the Pest side of the city, perfect for photography enthusiasts.

In addition to its cultural offerings, the Bazaar is home to several charming cafés and restaurants, where visitors can relax and enjoy local cuisine. The gardens themselves are a highlight, featuring meticulously maintained greenery and peaceful walking paths.

Tip: Visit the Bazaar in the early morning or late afternoon to avoid crowds and enjoy a more serene atmosphere. Don't miss the exhibitions inside the buildings, which often feature works by contemporary Hungarian artists. Combine your visit with a walk up to Buda Castle for a complete cultural and historical experience.

Address: Ybl Miklós tér 2-6, 1013 Budapest, Hungary
Website: www.varkertbazar.hu/en

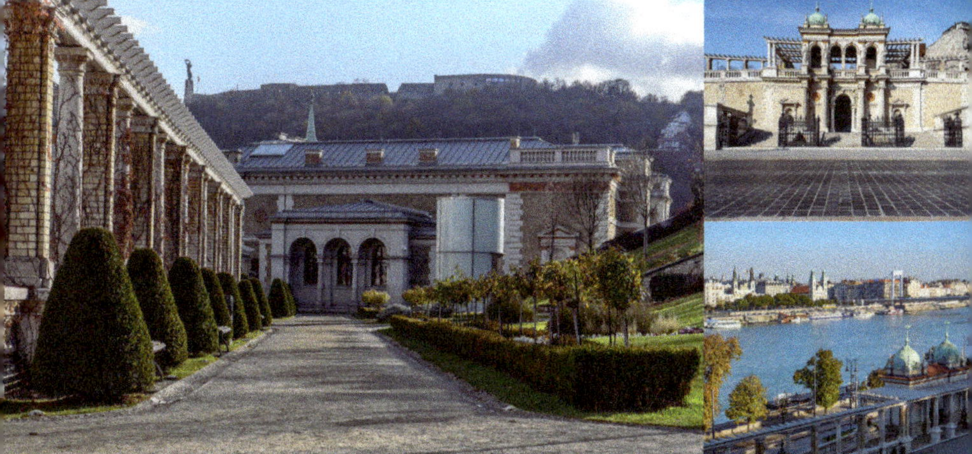

FLIPPERMÚZEUM (PINBALL MUSEUM)

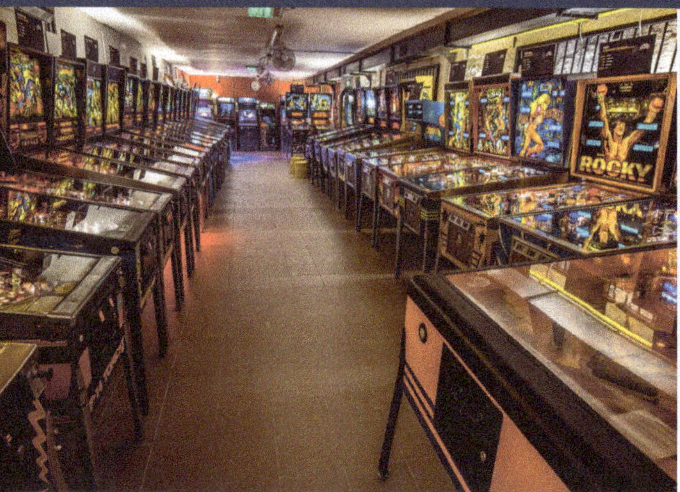
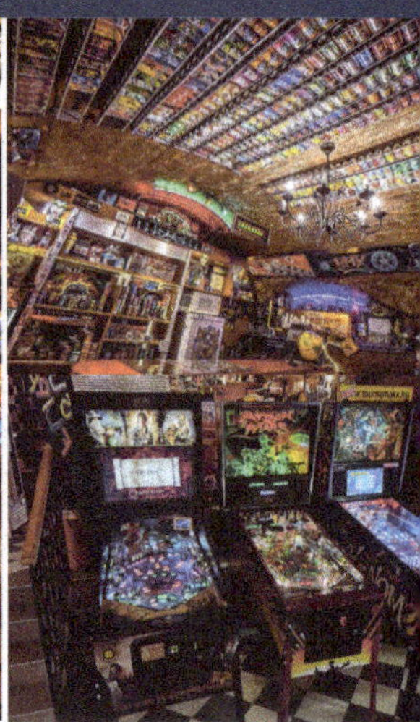

Flippermúzeum, or the Pinball Museum, is one of Budapest's most unique and entertaining attractions, offering a nostalgic journey through the history of pinball. Located in a basement in the heart of the city, this museum features the largest collection of pinball machines in Europe, with over 130 playable machines dating from the 19th century to the present day.

The museum's interactive nature allows visitors to play the machines, making it a hands-on experience that is fun for all ages. Each machine comes with information about its history and design, providing educational insights alongside the fun. From vintage wooden games to modern digital marvels, the collection spans decades of pinball innovation.

Flippermúzeum also includes rare and unique machines, such as early bagatelle tables and modern classics. The friendly staff are passionate about pinball and are happy to share their knowledge, ensuring visitors have an enjoyable and informative experience.

Tip: Plan to spend a few hours at the museum to fully enjoy the extensive collection and the opportunity to play on different machines. Visit on weekdays to avoid the weekend crowds and enjoy a more relaxed experience. The museum also has a small bar, so you can enjoy a drink while you play. Remember to bring cash, as card payments may not be accepted.

Address: Radnóti Miklós utca 18, 1137 Budapest, Hungary

Website: www.flippermuzeum.hu/en/

BUDAPEST EYE (FERRIS WHEEL)

The Budapest Eye, a prominent Ferris wheel located in Erzsébet Square, offers a unique and exhilarating way to view the city's stunning landscape. Standing at 65 meters tall, the Budapest Eye is one of the largest Ferris wheels in Europe, providing unparalleled panoramic views of Budapest's iconic landmarks, including the Buda Castle, St. Stephen's Basilica, and the Danube River.

Each rotation of the Ferris wheel lasts approximately 10 minutes, during which visitors can enjoy the city from a new perspective. The enclosed cabins are spacious and comfortable, making the experience enjoyable in any weather. At night, the Budapest Eye is illuminated, adding a festive and magical ambiance to the heart of the city.

Erzsébet Square itself is a lively area filled with green spaces, fountains, and cafés, making it a great spot to relax before or after your ride. The Budapest Eye is also conveniently located near other attractions, such as the Deák Ferenc Square and the shopping district along Váci Street.

Tip: For the best experience, ride the Budapest Eye at sunset or at night when the city is beautifully illuminated. Buy tickets in advance to avoid long lines, especially during peak tourist seasons. Combine your visit with a leisurely stroll around Erzsébet Square, where you can enjoy the vibrant atmosphere and local street performers.

Address: Erzsébet tér, 1051 Budapest, Hungary
Website: www.oriaskerek.com/en/

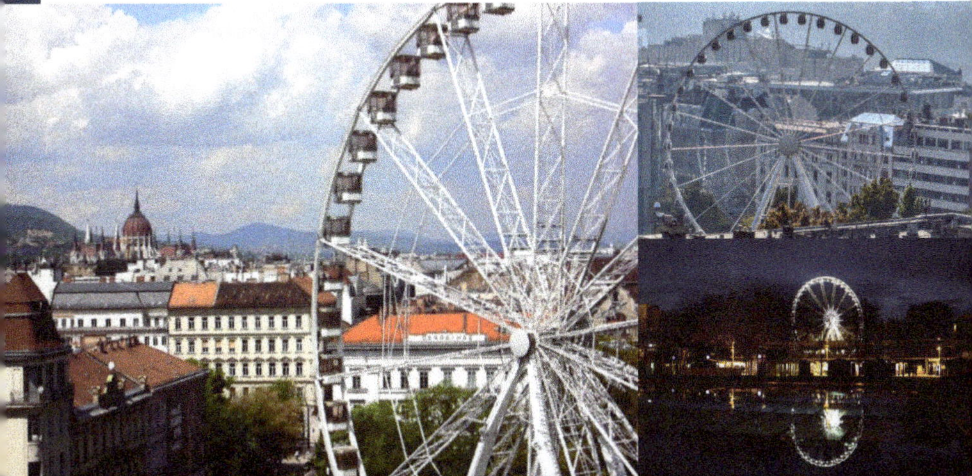

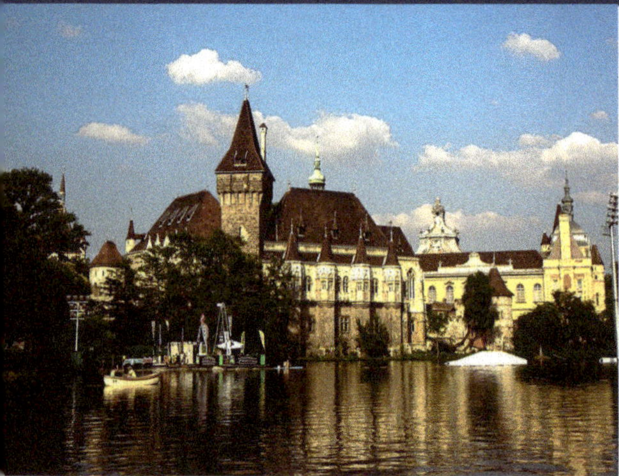
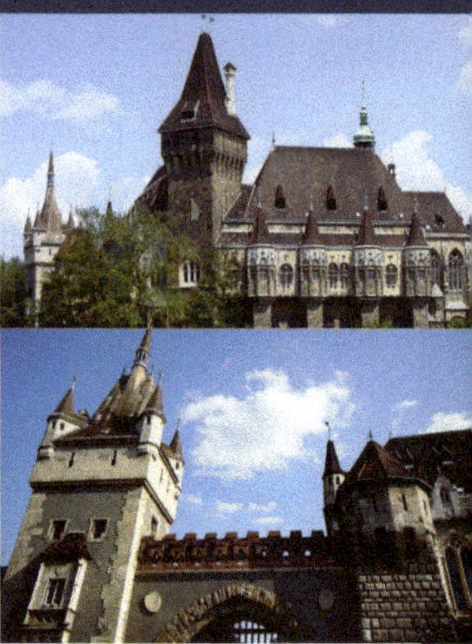

Vajdahunyad Castle, nestled in the picturesque City Park (Városliget), is one of Budapest's hidden gems, offering a blend of architectural styles and historical charm. Originally constructed for the 1896 Millennial Exhibition to celebrate Hungary's 1,000th anniversary, this enchanting castle is a replica of a Transylvanian fortress and incorporates Gothic, Romanesque, Renaissance, and Baroque elements.

The castle's fairy-tale appearance is complemented by its serene setting beside an artificial lake, which serves as an ice skating rink in winter and a boating lake in summer. Visitors can explore the castle's courtyards, towers, and the Chapel of Ják, a beautiful Romanesque-style church that is part of the complex. The castle also houses the Museum of Hungarian Agriculture, the largest of its kind in Europe, where you can learn about Hungary's agricultural history and traditions.

Vajdahunyad Castle is a perfect spot for leisurely walks, photo opportunities, and family outings. Its proximity to other City Park attractions, such as the Széchenyi Thermal Bath and the Budapest Zoo, makes it a convenient addition to your itinerary.

Tip: Visit the castle during the annual Hungarian Wine Festival in September for a unique cultural experience. Take a walk around the lake for different perspectives of the castle's stunning architecture. Don't forget to bring your camera to capture the picturesque views and intricate details of this magical landmark.

Address: Vajdahunyad vár, 1146 Budapest, Hungary

Website: www.mezogazdasagimuzeum.hu/home-en

MARGARET ISLAND

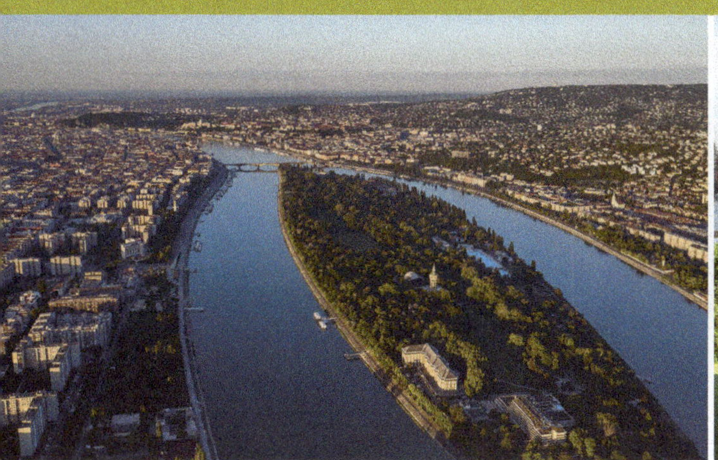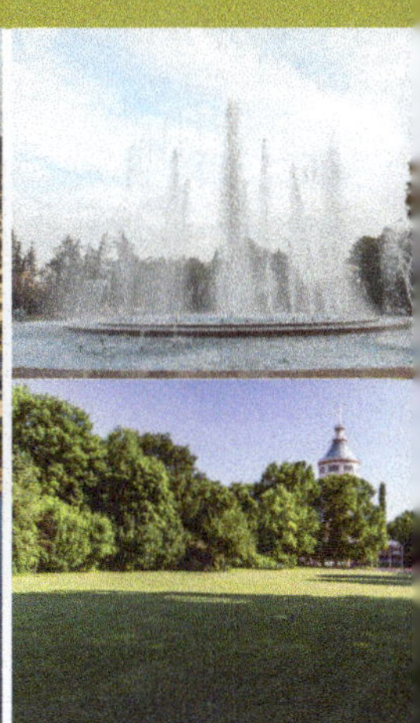

Margaret Island, located in the middle of the Danube River between Buda and Pest, is a lush, green oasis offering a peaceful retreat from the bustling city. Spanning 2.5 kilometers, this car-free island is a popular spot for both locals and tourists to relax, exercise, and enjoy nature. The island is named after Saint Margaret, who lived in a Dominican convent here in the 13th century.

The island boasts beautifully landscaped gardens, shaded walkways, and a variety of attractions. Key highlights include the Music Fountain, which offers a synchronized water and light show, and the Rose Garden, which bursts with color in the warmer months. Visitors can also explore the medieval ruins of the Franciscan church and the Dominican convent.

For active visitors, Margaret Island features running tracks, bike rentals, and an outdoor swimming complex. Families will enjoy the petting zoo and the Japanese Garden, complete with a small pond and picturesque bridges. The island's open spaces make it ideal for picnics, leisurely strolls, and sunbathing.

Tip: Rent a bike or a pedal-powered cart to explore the island comfortably. Plan your visit to coincide with the Music Fountain's performances for an enchanting experience. Pack a picnic and enjoy a leisurely day surrounded by nature.

Address: Margaret Island, 1138 Budapest, Hungary
Website: www.budapestinfo.hu/en/margaret-island-1

CITY PARK (VÁROSLIGET)

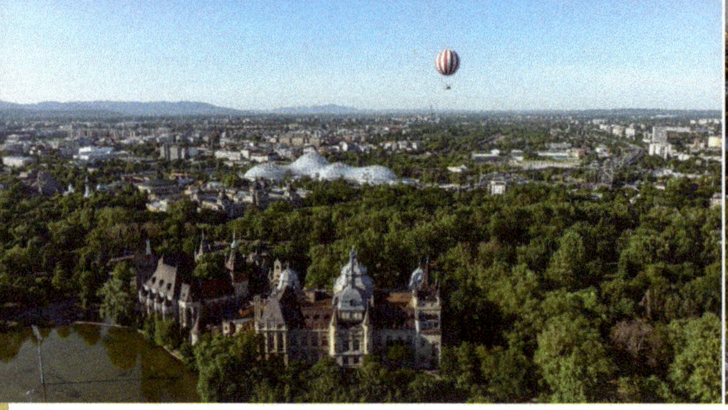

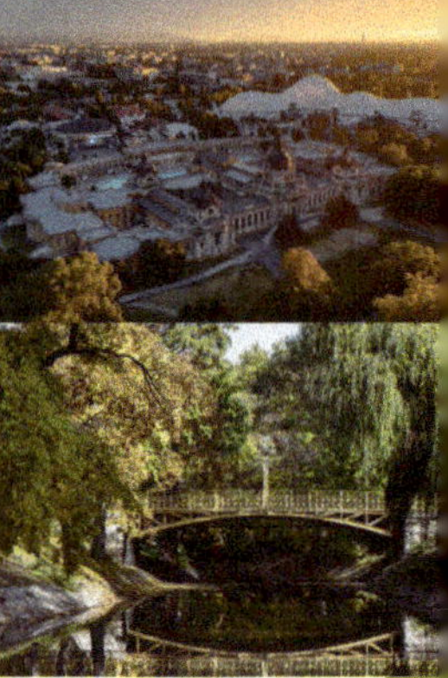

City Park, or Városliget, is Budapest's largest and most popular green space, offering a vast array of attractions and activities for visitors of all ages. Located in the heart of the city, this 302-acre park is a cultural and recreational hub, seamlessly blending nature with entertainment and history.

The park's highlights include the iconic Széchenyi Thermal Bath, one of Europe's largest spa complexes, where visitors can relax in the therapeutic waters. The park is also home to the Budapest Zoo & Botanical Garden, one of the oldest in the world, offering a delightful experience for families.

Vajdahunyad Castle, another gem within City Park, showcases a mix of architectural styles and houses the Museum of Hungarian Agriculture. The picturesque castle, surrounded by a tranquil lake, is a perfect spot for photos and leisurely walks. Additionally, the park features the Budapest Circus, offering entertaining performances throughout the year.

City Park is also the site of the Museum of Fine Arts and the Kunsthalle (Hall of Art), both of which host impressive art collections and exhibitions. For outdoor enthusiasts, the park offers running tracks, playgrounds, and expansive lawns ideal for picnics and relaxation.

Tip: Visit City Park early in the morning for a peaceful stroll or late in the afternoon to enjoy the lively atmosphere. Don't miss a ride on the historic Budapest Castle Hill Funicular for stunning views of the park and the city. Plan your visit to include a thermal bath

experience at Széchenyi for a truly relaxing day.
Address: Városliget, 1146 Budapest, Hungary
Website: www.budapestinfo.hu/en/spend-the-day-in-city-park-varosliget

BUDAPEST ZOO & BOTANICAL GARDEN

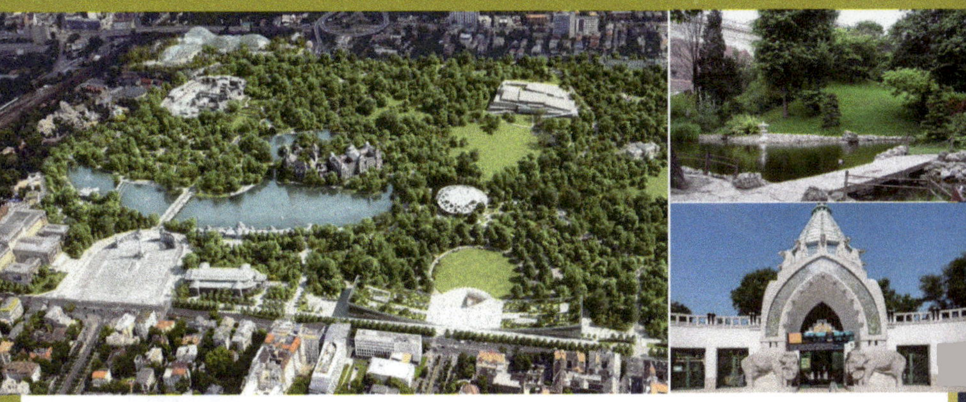

The Budapest Zoo & Botanical Garden, one of the oldest zoos in the world, is a must-visit attraction nestled within the expansive City Park (Városliget). Established in 1866, this historic zoo spans 18 hectares and is home to over 1,000 animal species and a stunning array of botanical specimens. Its beautiful Art Nouveau architecture and lush landscapes make it a delightful place for visitors of all ages.

The zoo's diverse collection includes exotic animals such as elephants, giraffes, lions, and tigers, as well as native Hungarian species. The Palm House, a grand glass structure, houses tropical plants and butterflies, providing a vibrant and immersive experience. Another highlight is the Australia House, where visitors can encounter kangaroos and other unique Australian wildlife.

In addition to the animal exhibits, the botanical garden features meticulously maintained gardens, rare plants, and themed sections like the Japanese Garden and the Rock Garden. The zoo also offers interactive experiences, such as petting zoos and feeding sessions, making it an engaging destination for families.

Tip: Plan to spend at least half a day exploring the zoo to fully appreciate its diverse attractions. Visit early in the morning to avoid crowds and see the animals at their most active. Don't miss the daily feeding sessions and educational programs, which provide deeper insights into the animals and their habitats. Consider bringing a picnic to enjoy in the scenic garden areas.

Address: Állatkerti krt. 6-12, 1146 Budapest, Hungary
Website: www.zoobudapest.com/en/home/

FÜVÉSZKERT BOTANICAL GARDEN

Füvészkert Botanical Garden, also known as the ELTE Botanical Garden, is a historic green space in Budapest, established in 1771. It spans over three hectares and houses more than 8,000 plant species, including exotic and rare varieties. The garden features a beautiful Victorian Palm House, a Japanese Garden, and tranquil ponds, making it an ideal spot for leisurely strolls and nature photography.

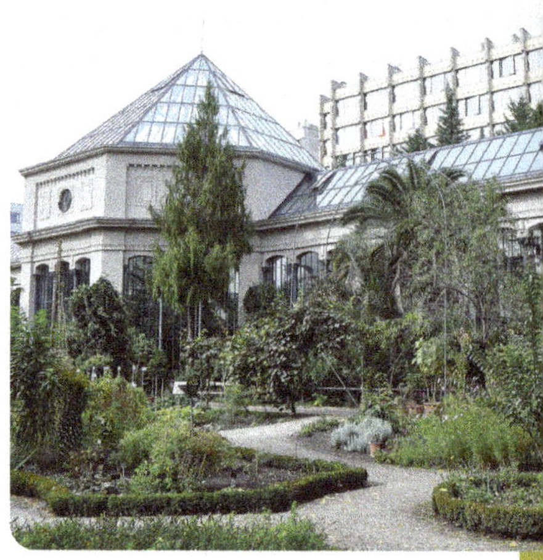

Tip: Visit in spring or early summer to see the garden in full bloom. Check the garden's schedule for guided tours and special

Address: Illés u. 25, 1083 Budapest, Hungary
Website: www.fuveszkert.org

ORCZY GARDEN

Orczy Garden, located in Budapest's Józsefváros district, is a serene public park with a rich history dating back to the 18th century. The garden features winding pathways, a tranquil pond, and picturesque bridges, offering a peaceful escape from the city's hustle. It's also home to the National Police Museum, adding a cultural dimension to your visit.

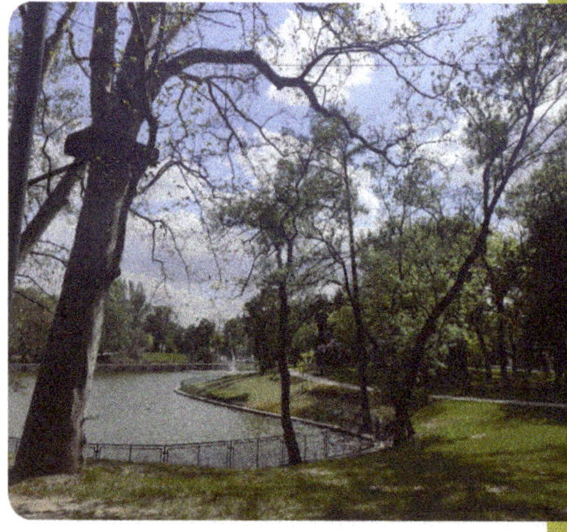

Tip: Visit early in the morning or late in the afternoon for a quieter experience. Bring a picnic to enjoy by the pond or explore the museum for an interesting cultural insight.

Address: Orczy út 1, 1089 Budapest, Hungary
Website: www.nhmus.hu/en/

ONYX RESTAURANT

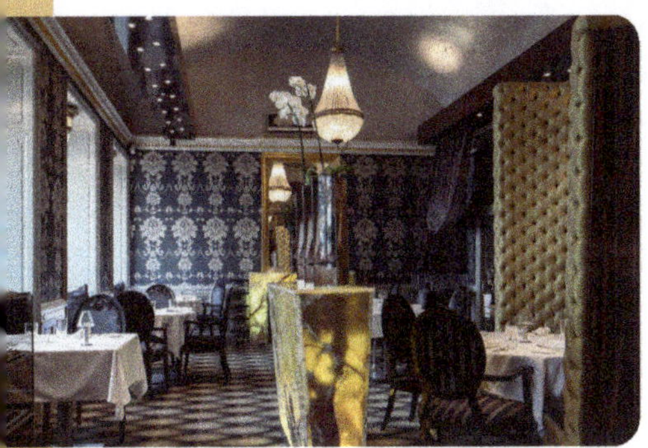

Onyx Restaurant, a Michelin-starred gem in Budapest, offers an exquisite dining experience with a modern twist on traditional Hungarian cuisine. The elegant interior, adorned with crystal chandeliers and plush seating, provides a luxurious ambiance for patrons. Onyx's menu features meticulously crafted dishes using the finest local ingredients, ensuring a memorable culinary journey.

Tip: Reservations are highly recommended due to the restaurant's popularity. Opt for the tasting menu to experience a diverse array of their finest creations paired with excellent Hungarian wines.

Address: Vörösmarty tér 7-8, 1051 Budapest, Hungary
Website: www.onyxmuhely.hu/en

COSTES RESTAURANT

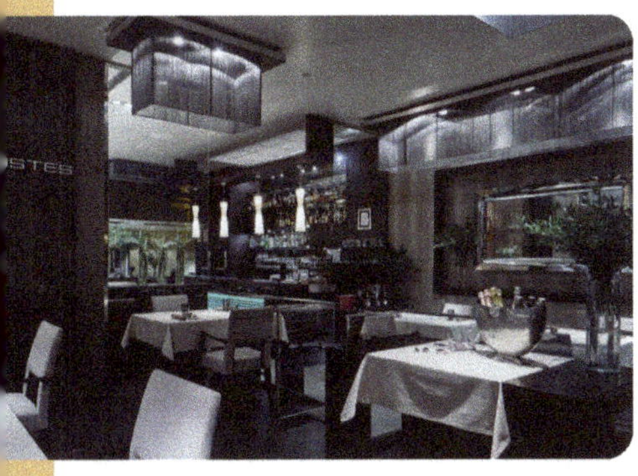

Costes Restaurant, Budapest's first Michelin-starred establishment, is renowned for its innovative approach to Hungarian and international cuisine. Located in the heart of the city, Costes offers a sophisticated dining atmosphere with contemporary décor.

The menu, curated by world-class chefs, features seasonal ingredients and artistic presentations that delight the senses.

Tip: Make a reservation well in advance to secure a table. Consider trying the chef's tasting menu for a comprehensive experience of their culinary artistry, complete with expertly paired wine selections.

Address: Ráday u. 4, 1092 Budapest, Hungary
Website: www.costesrestaurant.hu/en/

NEW YORK CAFÉ

New York Café, often referred to as the "most beautiful café in the world," is a historic gem located in the New York Palace. Its opulent interior, featuring stunning frescoes, crystal chandeliers, and gold detailing, transports guests to a bygone era of grandeur. The menu offers a delightful selection of Hungarian and international dishes, as well as exquisite pastries and coffee.

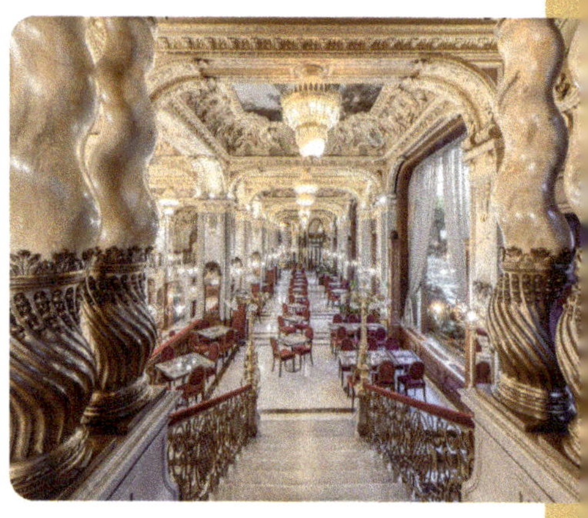

Tip: Arrive early to avoid long waits, as this popular spot can get crowded. Indulge in their famous New York coffee and a decadent dessert for a truly memorable experience.

Address: Erzsébet krt. 9-11, 1073 Budapest, Hungary
Website: www.newyorkcafe.hu/en/

BORS GASZTROBAR

Bors GasztroBar is a beloved local favorite known for its creative street food and vibrant atmosphere. Located near the bustling Kazinczy Street, this small eatery offers a diverse menu of gourmet soups, sandwiches, and pastas, all made with fresh, high-quality ingredients. The friendly staff and quirky decor add to its charm.

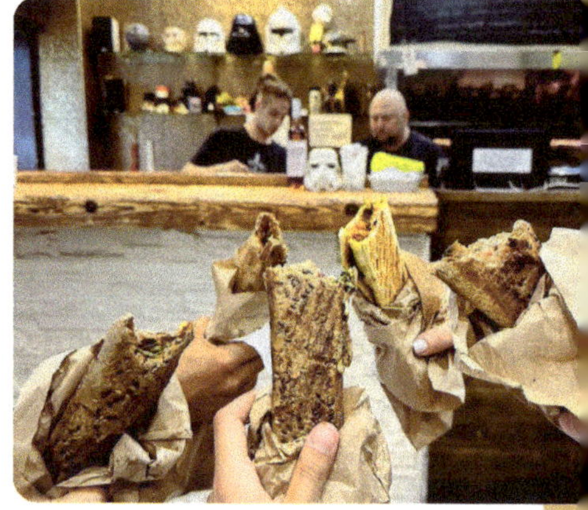

Tip: Try the daily specials for a unique culinary experience. Be prepared for a queue during peak hours, but the delicious and innovative food is well worth the wait.

Address: Kazinczy u. 10, 1075 Budapest, Hungary
Website: www.facebook.com/BorsGasztroBar

GOULASH

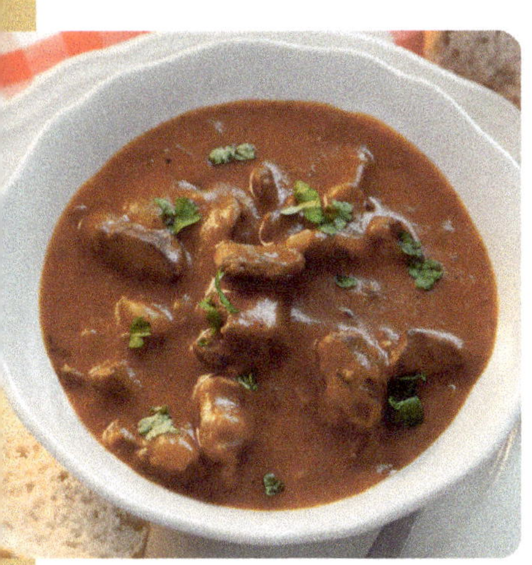

Goulash, Hungary's most famous culinary export, is a hearty stew that perfectly embodies the rich flavors of Hungarian cuisine. This traditional dish is made by slow-cooking beef with onions, paprika, tomatoes, and bell peppers, resulting in a deeply flavorful and warming meal. Often served with potatoes or homemade noodles, goulash is a staple in Hungarian households and a must-try for visitors.

The use of Hungarian paprika gives goulash its distinctive taste, making it a unique and authentic experience. **Where to Try**: "Hungarikum Bisztró" is renowned for its delicious and authentic goulash. **Location**: Steindl Imre u. 13, 1051 Budapest, Hungary; **Tip**: Pair your goulash with a glass of robust Hungarian red wine, such as Kadarka, to enhance the dish's rich flavors.

KÜRTŐSKALÁCS

Kürtőskalács, or chimney cake, is a beloved Hungarian pastry that tantalizes with its sweet, caramelized crust and soft, fluffy interior. Made by wrapping dough around a spit, baking it over an open fire, and then rolling it in sugar, this treat is often sprinkled with cinnamon, nuts, or coconut for added flavor. Originating from Transylvania, kürtőskalács is a popular street food and festival favorite, offering a delightful taste of Hungarian tradition.

Where to Try: "Molnár's Kürtőskalács" is famous for its authentic and mouthwatering chimney cakes. **Location**: Váci u. 31, 1052 Budapest, Hungary
Tip: Enjoy your kürtőskalács fresh and warm from the oven for the best taste. Pair it with a cup of coffee or hot chocolate for a perfect sweet treat.

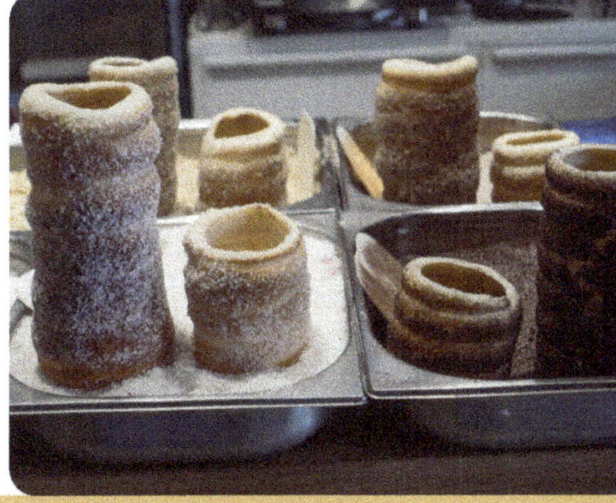

TOKAJI WINE

Tokaji Wine, often referred to as the "Wine of Kings and the King of Wines," is a prestigious Hungarian dessert wine with a rich history dating back centuries. Produced in the Tokaj region of northeastern Hungary, this sweet wine is made from Furmint and Hárslevelű grapes affected by noble rot, which concentrates the sugars and flavors. Tokaji Aszú, the most famous variety, boasts complex flavors of apricot, honey, and spices, offering a luxurious finish to any meal.

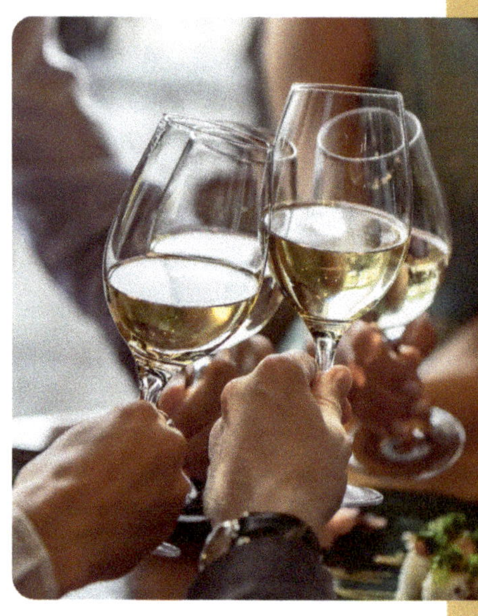

Where to Try: "Borbíróság" is celebrated for its excellent selection of Tokaji wines. **Location**: Csarnok tér 5, 1093 Budapest, Hungary
Tip: Enjoy Tokaji wine slightly chilled and pair it with blue cheese or foie gras to complement its sweet, rich flavors.

LÁNGOS

Lángos, a quintessential Hungarian street food, is a deep-fried dough typically topped with garlic, sour cream, and grated cheese. This savory delight is crispy on the outside and soft on the inside, making it a perfect snack or quick meal. Lángos is a beloved treat at fairs and markets, offering a delicious taste of Hungarian culinary tradition.

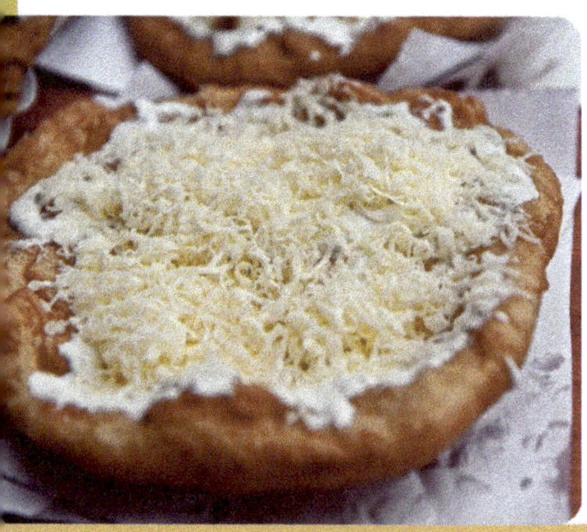

Where to Try: "Retró Lángos Büfé" is renowned for serving some of the best lángos in Budapest. **Location**: Arany János u. 31, 1051 Budapest, Hungary
Tip: Try the classic garlic, sour cream, and cheese topping for an authentic experience. Pair your lángos with a cold beer or a refreshing glass of lemonade for the perfect street food meal.

DOBOS TORTE

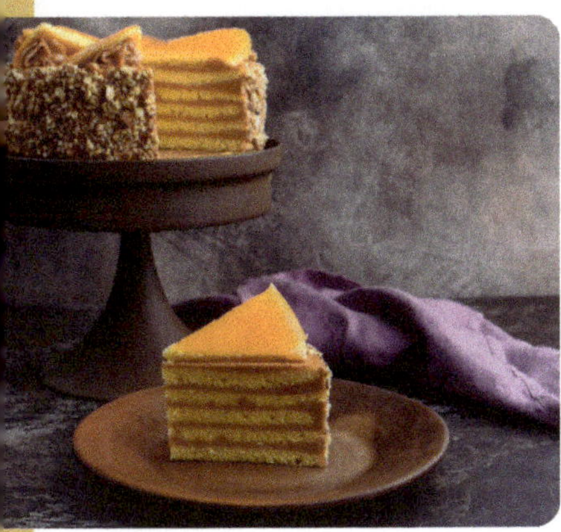

Dobos Torte is a classic Hungarian dessert that epitomizes the elegance of Hungarian pastry arts. This layered sponge cake, filled with rich chocolate buttercream and topped with a caramel glaze, was created by József C. Dobos in the late 19th century. The cake's unique appearance and decadent taste make it a favorite at celebrations and patisseries across Budapest.

Where to Try: "Gerbeaud Café" is famous for its exquisite Dobos Torte and other traditional Hungarian desserts.
Location: Vörösmarty tér 7-8, 1051 Budapest, Hungary
Tip: Pair a slice of Dobos Torte with a cup of strong Hungarian coffee to balance the sweetness of the cake. Visit Gerbeaud Café in the afternoon to enjoy a relaxed atmosphere and avoid the busiest times.

PÁLINKA

Pálinka is a traditional Hungarian fruit brandy, known for its strong, aromatic flavors. Made from various fruits such as plums, apricots, and pears, this potent spirit is an integral part of Hungarian culture and hospitality. Pálinka is enjoyed as a digestive, and its high alcohol content and fruity notes make it a unique experience for spirit enthusiasts.

Where to Try: "Pálinka Museum" offers tastings of high-quality pálinka varieties, along with insights into its production and history.
Location: Király u. 20, 1061 Budapest, Hungary
Tip: Savor pálinka in small sips to fully appreciate its complex flavors. Consider visiting the Pálinka Museum for a guided tasting session and to learn more about this iconic Hungarian spirit.

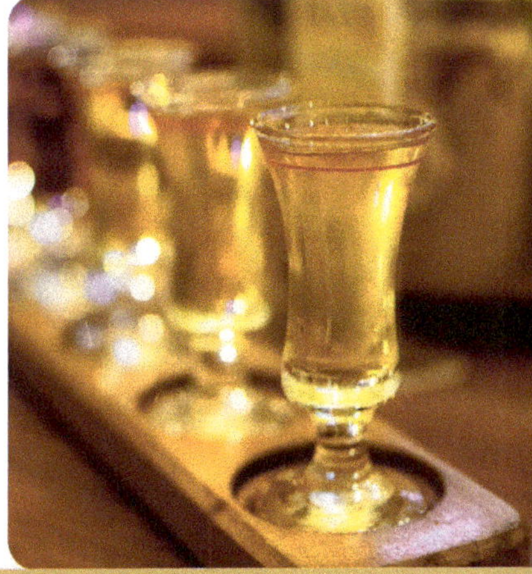

VÁCI STREET

Váci Street is Budapest's premier shopping destination, stretching from Vörösmarty Square to the Great Market Hall. This bustling pedestrian street is lined with an array of shops, boutiques, and cafés, offering everything from high-end fashion to unique souvenirs. As you stroll along Váci Street, you'll encounter international brands, local designers,

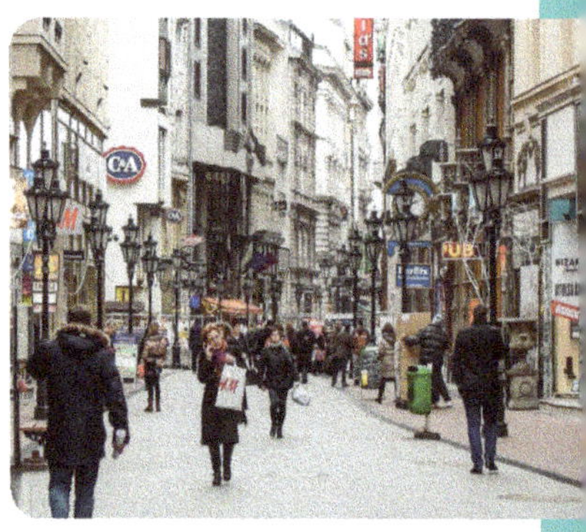

and charming gift shops, making it a must-visit for any shopping enthusiast. **Tip**: Visit early in the morning or late in the afternoon to avoid the crowds. Don't miss the side streets for hidden gems and local artisan shops.

Address: Váci utca, 1052 Budapest, Hungary
Website:
https://en.wikipedia.org/wiki/V%C3%A1ci_Street

WESTEND CITY CENTER

WestEnd City Center is one of Budapest's largest and most modern shopping malls, offering a comprehensive shopping experience with over 400 stores. Located next to the Nyugati Railway Station, the mall features international brands, local boutiques, a multiplex cinema, and a variety of dining options. Its expansive layout and contemporary design make it a popular destination for both locals and tourists.

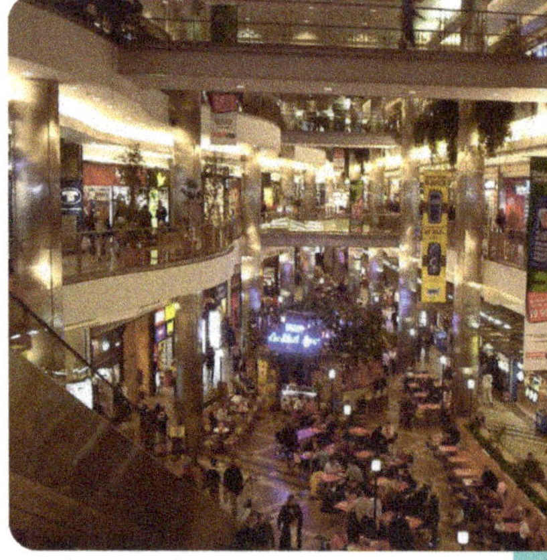

Tip: Visit the rooftop garden for a relaxing break from shopping and enjoy panoramic views of the city. The mall is busiest on weekends, so plan your visit during weekdays for a more leisurely experience.

Address: Váci út 1-3, 1062 Budapest, Hungary
Website: www.westend.hu/en

ANDRASSY AVENUE

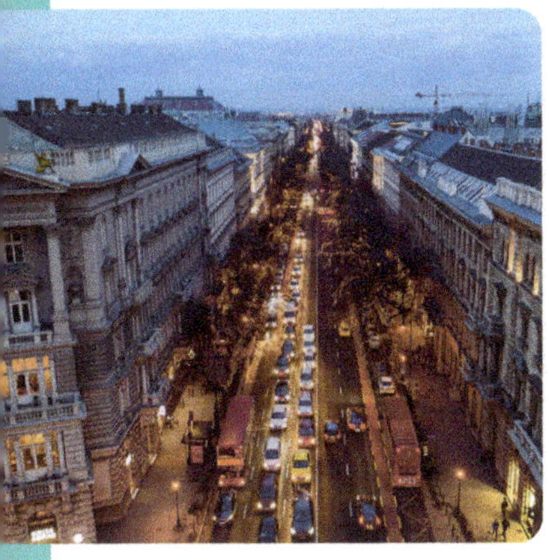

Andrássy Avenue, a UNESCO World Heritage site, is Budapest's most elegant boulevard, renowned for its high-end shopping and stunning architecture. Stretching from the city center to Heroes' Square, this historic street is lined with luxury boutiques, designer stores, and charming cafés. Andrássy Avenue offers a sophisticated shopping experience amidst beautifully preserved 19th-century buildings.

Tip: Combine your shopping trip with a visit to nearby attractions like the Hungarian State Opera House or the House of Terror Museum. Take a leisurely stroll to fully appreciate the avenue's architectural beauty and vibrant atmosphere.

Address: Andrássy út, 1061 Budapest, Hungary
Website: www.budapestinfo.hu/en/andrassy-avenue
Image credit: welovebudapest.com

ECSERI FLEA MARKET

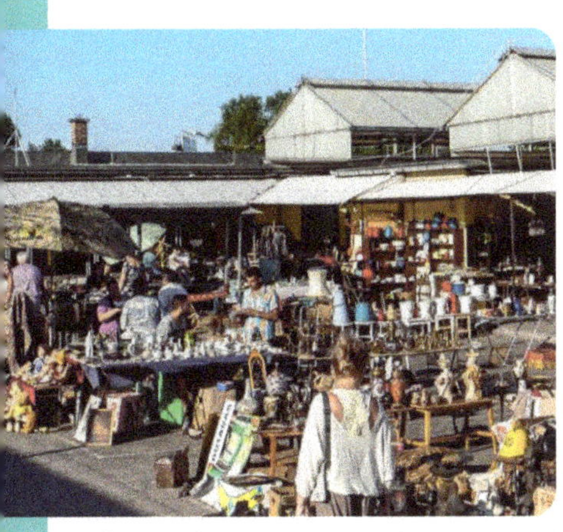

Ecseri Flea Market is Budapest's largest and most famous flea market, offering a treasure trove of antiques, collectibles, and unique finds. From vintage furniture and jewelry to rare books and memorabilia, this bustling market is a paradise for bargain hunters and history enthusiasts. It's the perfect place to discover hidden gems and souvenirs that tell a story.

Tip: Arrive early for the best selection and be prepared to haggle for the best prices. Bring cash, as many vendors may not accept credit cards.

Address: Nagykőrösi út 156, 1194 Budapest, Hungary
Website: www.piaconline.hu/en/nagykorosi-street-flea-market/
Image credit: piaconline.hu

ARENA MALL

Arena Mall is one of Budapest's premier shopping destinations, featuring a wide range of international and local brands, dining options, and entertainment facilities. Located near the Keleti Railway Station, this modern shopping center offers everything from fashion and electronics to beauty products and home goods. Its spacious layout and contemporary design make for a comfortable shopping experience. **Tip**: Visit during weekdays to avoid the weekend crowds. Take advantage of the mall's dining options for a meal or

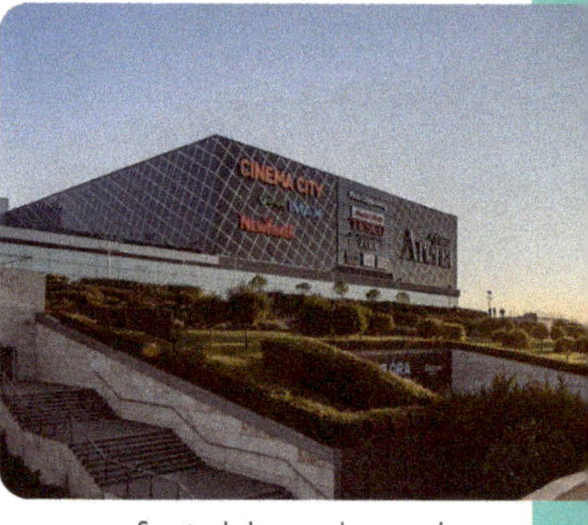

coffee break between shopping. Don't miss the cinema for a movie after your shopping spree.

Address: Kerepesi út 9, 1087 Budapest, Hungary
Website: www.arenamall.hu/en

MAMMUT SHOPPING CENTER

Mammut Shopping Center is a popular retail complex located in the Buda side of Budapest. Split into two interconnected buildings, Mammut I and Mammut II, the mall offers a wide range of shopping options including international and local brands, electronics, home

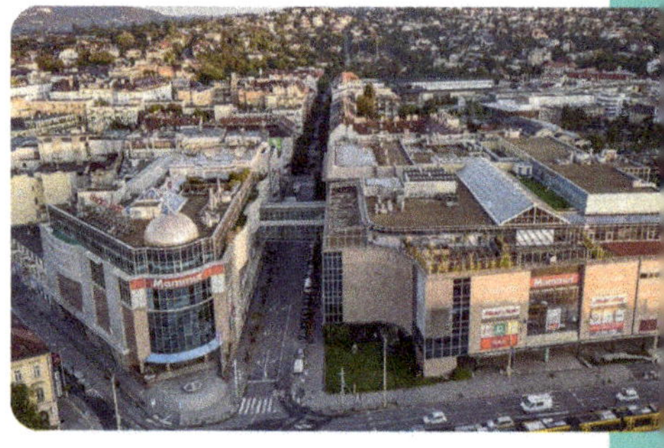

goods, and beauty products. In addition to its extensive retail selection, Mammut features a variety of dining options, a fitness center, and a cinema, making it a convenient and enjoyable destination for shopping and entertainment.

Tip: Take advantage of the mall's ample parking and easy access to public transportation. Visit during the week to avoid the weekend rush, and explore both buildings to fully experience the

variety of shops and services offered.
Address: Lövőház u. 2-6, 1024 Budapest, Hungary
Website: www.mammut.hu/en

FAMILY-FRIENDLY ACTIVITIES

BUDAPEST ZOO

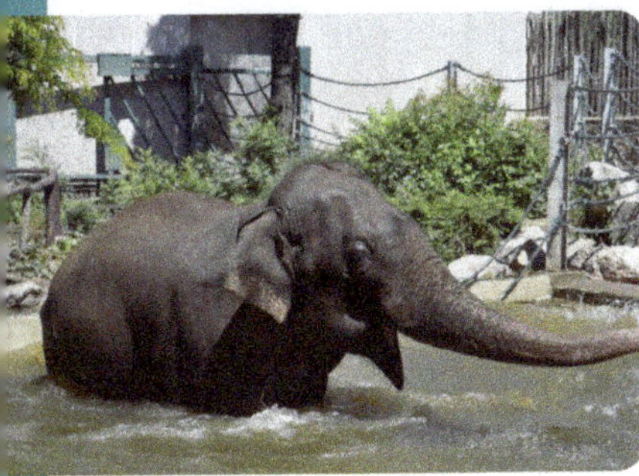

The Budapest Zoo & Botanical Garden, one of the oldest zoos in the world, offers an engaging experience for families with over 1,000 animal species and lush botanical displays. Located in City Park, it features interactive exhibits, a petting zoo, and themed gardens, making it a perfect destination for a fun and educational day out.

Tip: Plan to spend at least half a day exploring the zoo to fully enjoy its attractions. Arrive early to avoid crowds and catch the animals at their most active. Don't miss the daily feeding sessions and educational programs.

Address: Állatkerti krt. 6-12, 1146 Budapest, Hungary
Website: www.zoobudapest.com/en/home/

CHILDREN'S RAILWAY IN BUDA HILLS

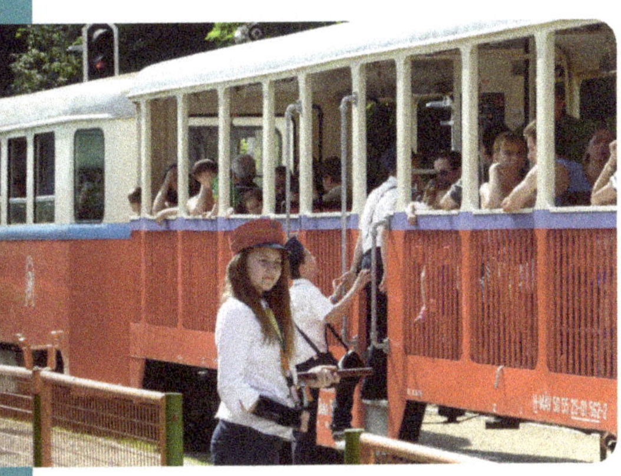

The Children's Railway in Buda Hills offers a unique and fun experience for families. Operated by children under adult supervision, this narrow-gauge railway winds through scenic forests and hills, providing stunning views and access to several hiking trails and picnic spots. It's a delightful adventure for kids and adults alike.

Tip: Combine the train ride with a visit to the nearby Normafa for a picnic or a hike. Check the timetable in advance to plan your trip and enjoy the full scenic route.

Address: Budapest, Gyermekvasúthoz vezető út 5, 1021 Hungary
Website: www.gyermekvasut.hu/en/home/

PALATINUS STRAND

Palatinus Strand is one of Budapest's largest and most popular outdoor water parks, located on Margaret Island. Featuring a variety of pools, including wave and thermal pools, as well as water slides and a children's playground, Palatinus offers a fun-filled day for the entire family. The beautiful park setting provides ample space for picnics and relaxation.

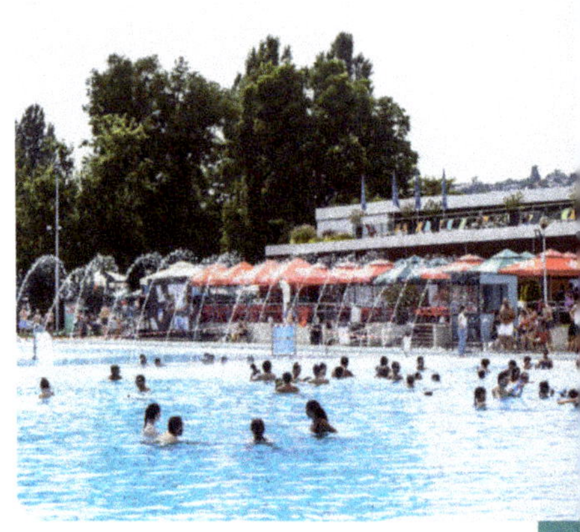

Tip: Visit early in the morning to secure a good spot by the pools. Bring sunscreen and plenty of water, as the outdoor areas can get quite sunny during peak hours.

Address: Budapest, Soó Rezső stny. 1, 1007 Hungary
Website: https://en.palatinusstrand.hu/

TROPICARIUM

Tropicarium, also known as the "Budapest Zoo in the Sea," is an exciting indoor aquarium and zoo located in the Campona Shopping Mall. It features a wide variety of aquatic life, including sharks, rays, and exotic fish, as well as tropical birds, reptiles, and monkeys. The highlight is

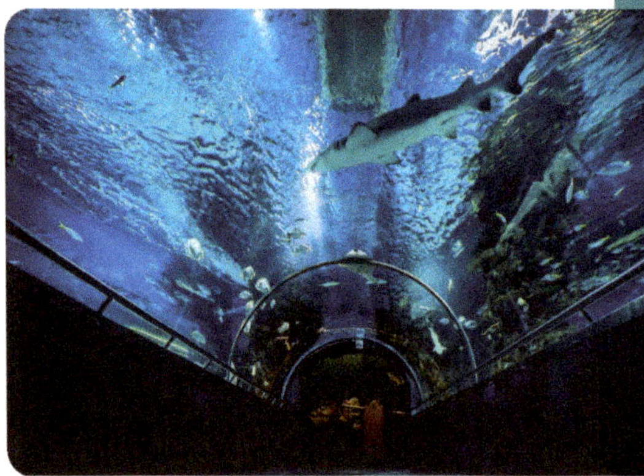

the 12-meter-long shark tunnel, where visitors can walk through and see sharks swimming overhead.

Tip: Plan your visit around the feeding times for an extra engaging experience. Don't forget to bring a camera for unique underwater photos and to capture the colorful marine life.

Address: Nagytétényi út 37-43, 1222 Budapest, Hungary
Website: www.tropicarium.hu/en/home/

BUDAPEST CIRCUS

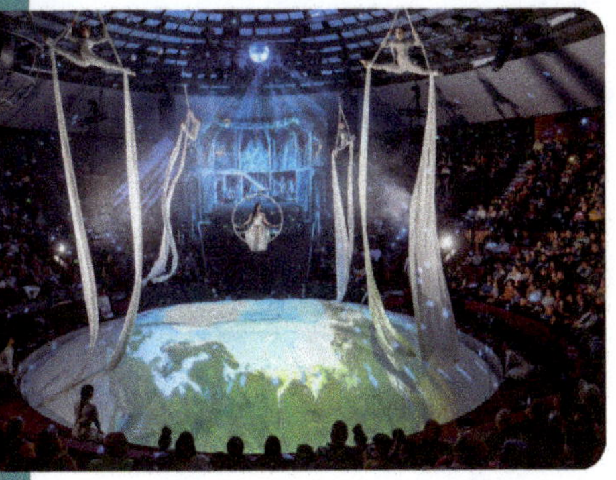

The Budapest Circus, also known as the Capital Circus of Budapest, is a traditional circus offering spectacular performances that delight audiences of all ages. Located in City Park, it features acrobats, clowns, animal acts, and various international circus artists. The historic venue and entertaining shows make it a must-visit for families seeking a fun and memorable outing.

Tip: Check the schedule in advance and book tickets online to ensure good seats. Arrive early to explore the nearby attractions in City Park, such as the Budapest Zoo and Széchenyi Thermal Bath.

Address: Állatkerti krt. 12/a, 1146 Budapest, Hungary
Website: www.fnc.hu/stars-like-pins-on-the-sky/

AQUAWORLD BUDAPEST

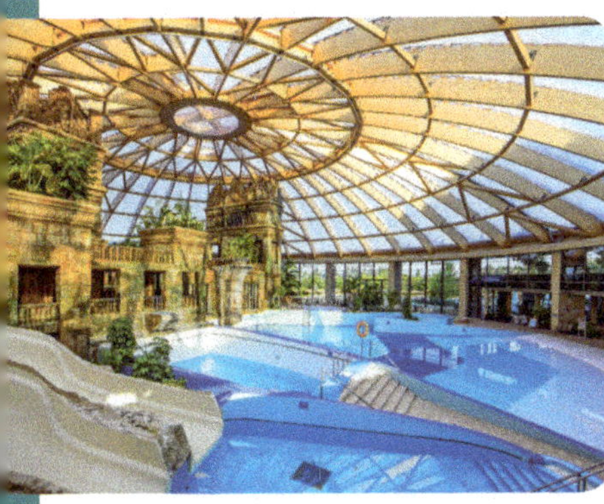

Aquaworld Budapest is one of Europe's largest indoor water parks, offering a fantastic family-friendly experience with a variety of pools, water slides, and adventure activities. The park features a wave pool, a surf pool, and a separate area for toddlers, ensuring fun for all ages. The exotic-themed environment provides a perfect escape for families looking to relax and enjoy water-based entertainment.

Tip: Visit on weekdays for a quieter experience. Bring swimwear and towels, and consider booking tickets online in advance to avoid long lines and ensure entry during peak times.

Address: Íves út 16, 1044 Budapest, Hungary
Website: www.aquaworldresort.hu/en

BUDAPEST BY NIGHT

ILLUMINATED MONUMENTS AND EVENING STROLLS

CHAIN BRIDGE

Chain Bridge, or Széchenyi Lánchíd, is one of Budapest's most iconic landmarks, offering a stunning view when illuminated at night. Connecting Buda and Pest across the Danube River, the bridge's lights create a picturesque reflection on the water, making it a perfect spot for an evening stroll. Walking across

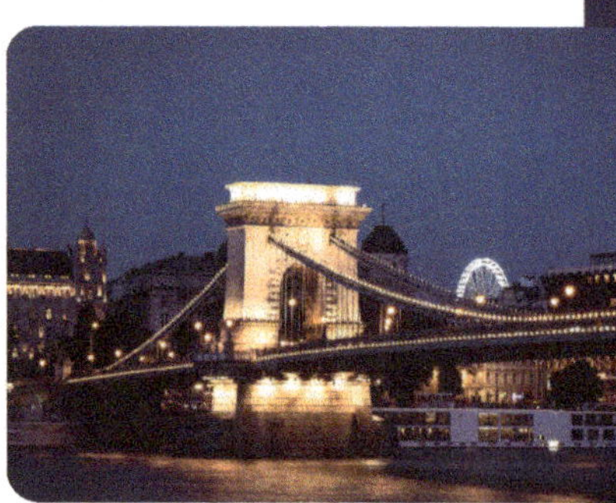

the bridge, you can enjoy panoramic views of the city, including the Hungarian Parliament Building and Buda Castle.

Tip: Visit just after sunset for the best photo opportunities and a magical atmosphere. Combine your walk with a visit to the nearby

Danube Promenade for a full evening experience.
Address: Széchenyi Lánchíd, 1051 Budapest, Hungary
Website: www.budapestinfo.hu/en/chain-bridge

HUNGARIAN PARLIAMENT BUILDING

The Hungarian Parliament Building is breathtaking at night, with its Gothic Revival architecture beautifully illuminated against the night sky. Situated along the Danube River, the building's lights highlight its intricate details and grand stature, offering a spectacular view from both Buda and Pest. An evening stroll along the river

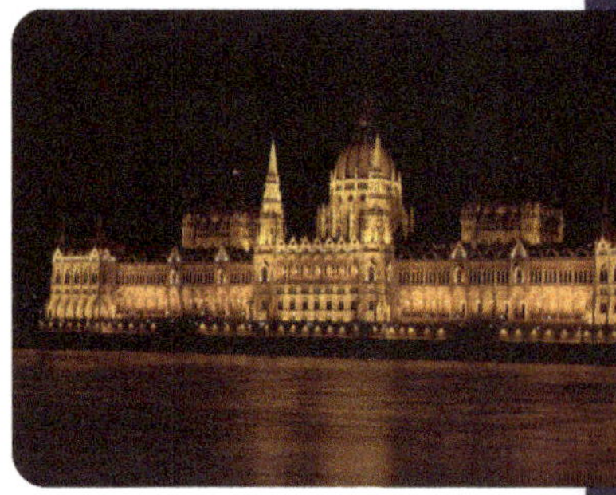

provides a perfect vantage point to admire this architectural masterpiece.

Tip: For the best views, walk along the Danube Promenade on the Pest side or cross the Chain Bridge to view it from Buda. Consider taking a nighttime river cruise for an unparalleled perspective.
Address: Kossuth Lajos tér 1-3, 1055 Budapest, Hungary
Website: www.parlament.hu/en/web/visitors

ST. STEPHEN'S BASILICA

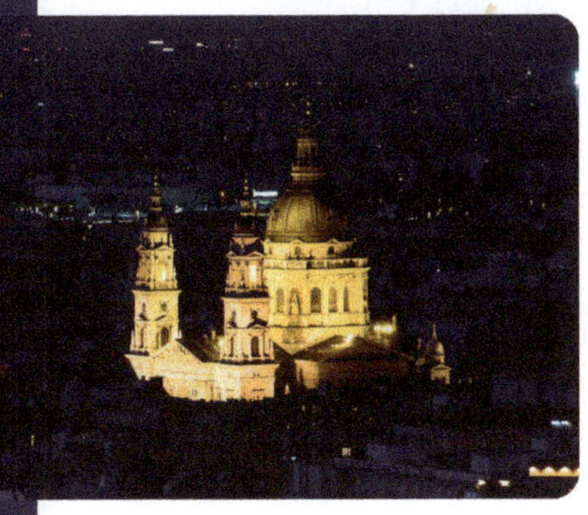

St. Stephen's Basilica, a neoclassical marvel, is even more enchanting when illuminated at night. The grand facade and dome are beautifully lit, creating a serene and majestic atmosphere in the heart of Budapest. The square in front of the basilica is a perfect spot for an evening stroll, where you can admire the stunning architecture and enjoy the vibrant yet tranquil ambiance.

Tip: Visit the nearby rooftop bars for a panoramic view of the illuminated basilica. Evening concerts often held inside offer a unique way to experience the basilica's beauty and acoustics.

Address: Szent István tér 1, 1051 Budapest, Hungary
Website: www.bazilika.biz/en

BUDA CASTLE

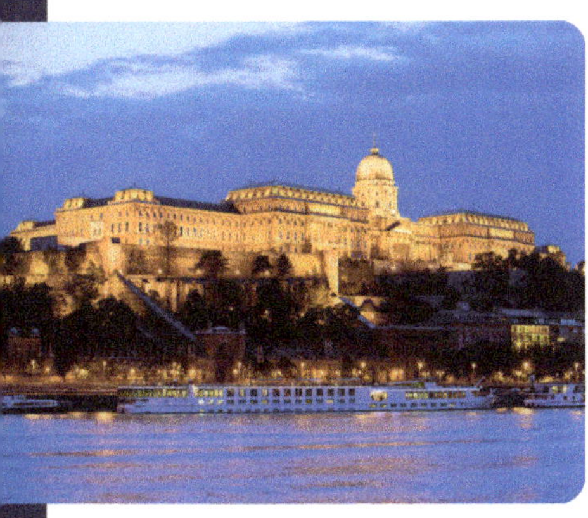

Buda Castle, perched on Castle Hill, offers a magical view when illuminated at night. The historic castle complex, glowing against the dark sky, provides a breathtaking backdrop for an evening stroll along the castle grounds or the Danube Promenade. The lights highlight its Baroque architecture, making it a must-see sight after sunset.

Tip: Take the funicular up to the castle for a scenic ride, then enjoy a leisurely walk around the grounds. The view of the illuminated city from the castle is spectacular, especially from Fisherman's Bastion.

Address: Szent György tér 2, 1014 Budapest, Hungary
Website: www.budacastlebudapest.com

SZIMPLA KERT

Szimpla Kert is Budapest's most famous ruin pub, offering a unique nightlife experience in a quirky, eclectic setting. Housed in a dilapidated building, the pub features mismatched furniture, graffiti-covered walls, and a variety of themed rooms. Szimpla Kert is known for its vibrant atmosphere, live music,

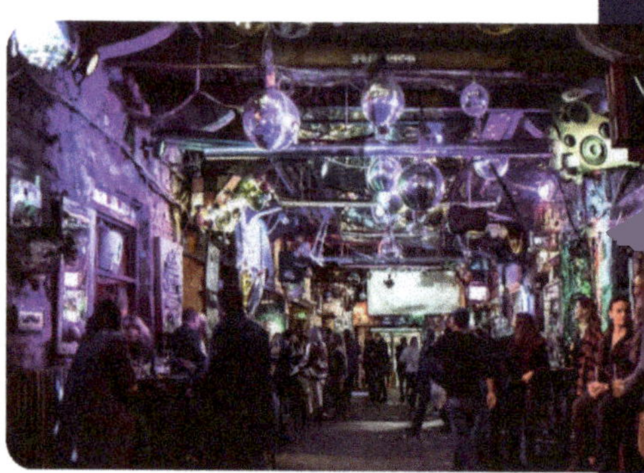

and a wide selection of drinks, making it a must-visit spot for a memorable night out.

Tip: Visit on a Sunday for the popular Szimpla Farmers' Market, where you can enjoy local produce and snacks in the unique ruin pub setting.

Address: Kazinczy u. 14, 1075 Budapest, Hungary
Website: www.szimpla.hu

INSTANT-FOGAS

Instant-Fogas is one of Budapest's largest and most popular ruin pub complexes, combining two legendary venues. This sprawling nightlife destination features multiple dance floors, themed rooms, and outdoor courtyards. With a diverse music lineup ranging from electronic to rock, Instant-

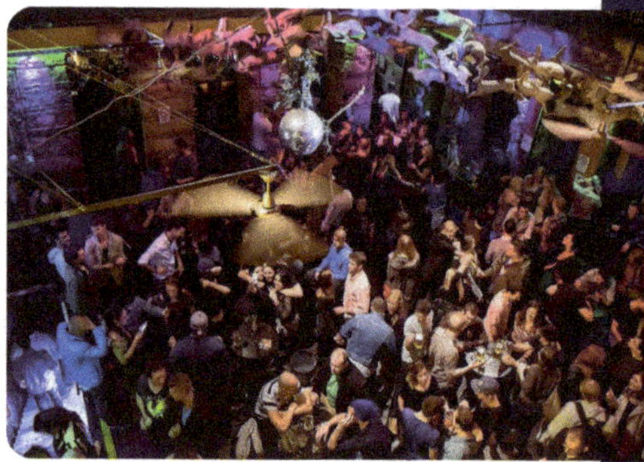

Fogas offers something for everyone, ensuring an unforgettable night out in Budapest's vibrant ruin pub scene.

Tip: Arrive early to explore the different rooms and find your favorite spot before the crowds arrive. Check their website for

upcoming events and themed parties.
Address: Akácfa u. 49-51, 1073 Budapest, Hungary
Website: www.instant-fogas.com

360 BAR

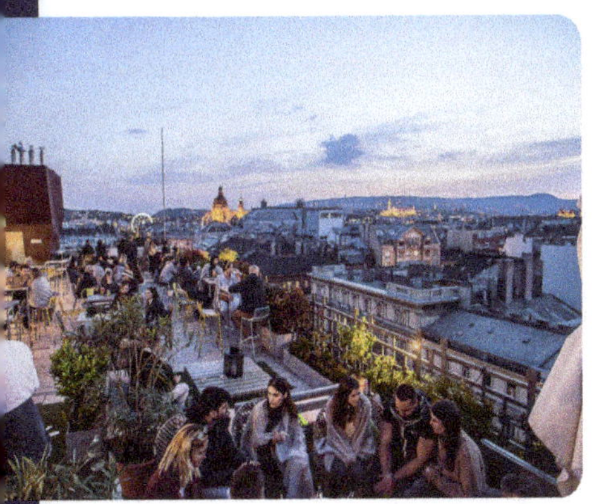

360 Bar is a rooftop bar offering stunning panoramic views of Budapest. Located atop a historic building on Andrássy Avenue, this trendy spot is known for its chic ambiance, creative cocktails, and delicious food. The bar's open-air terrace, complete with cozy igloos in the winter, provides the perfect setting for a memorable night out, whether you're enjoying the sunset or the city lights.

Tip: Arrive early to secure a good spot and enjoy the sunset. Make a reservation if you plan to visit during peak hours, especially in the summer months.

Address: Andrássy út 39, 1061 Budapest, Hungary
Website: www.360bar.hu

AKVÁRIUM KLUB

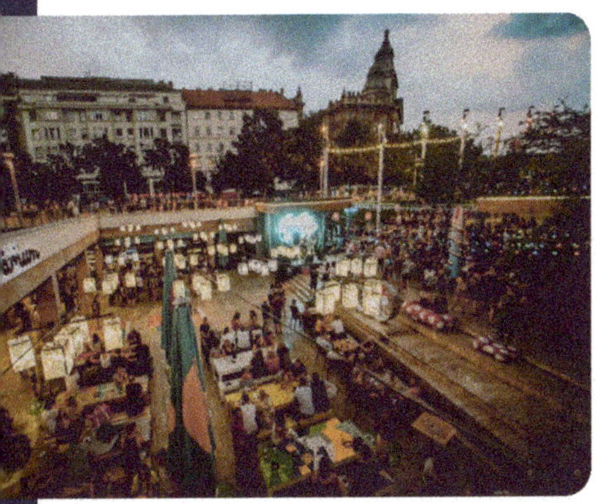

Akvárium Klub, located in the heart of Budapest, is a versatile nightlife venue offering live music, DJ sets, and cultural events. The club features multiple stages, an outdoor terrace, and a large pool that creates a unique underwater ambiance. Known for its vibrant atmosphere and diverse entertainment, Akvárium Klub is a favorite among locals and tourists alike for a dynamic night out.

Tip: Check the event schedule on their website to catch your favorite performers. Enjoy a drink on the terrace before heading inside to experience the club's lively atmosphere.

Address: Erzsébet tér 12, 1051 Budapest, Hungary
Website: www.akvariumklub.hu/en/

ÖTKERT

Ötkert is one of Budapest's most popular nightclubs, offering a vibrant nightlife experience in a stylish, converted ruin pub. Located near St. Stephen's Basilica, Ötkert features multiple dance floors, a spacious courtyard, and a diverse music lineup that includes everything from electronic to hip-hop.

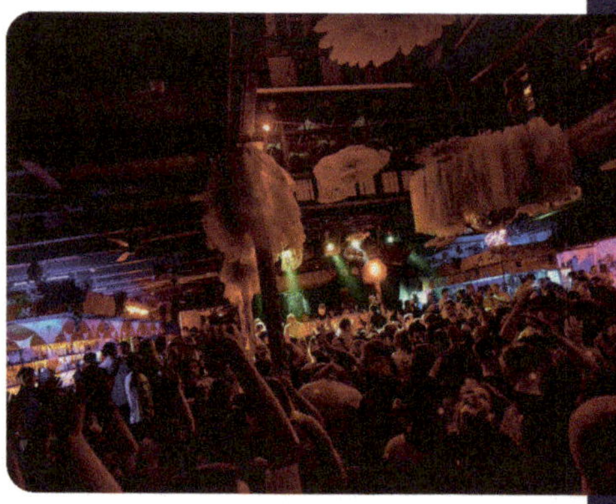

The club's lively atmosphere and chic design make it a favorite destination for locals and tourists alike looking to dance the night away. **Tip**: Arrive before midnight to avoid long lines and enjoy a more relaxed entry. Check their website for special events and themed nights.

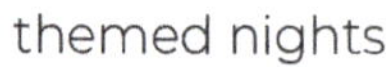

Address: Zrínyi u. 4, 1051 Budapest, Hungary
Website: www.otkert.hu/en/

PEACHES AND CREAM CLUB

Peaches and Cream Club is a lively nightclub in Budapest's Jewish Quarter, known for its energetic atmosphere and diverse music. The club features multiple dance floors, VIP areas, and a stylish interior. With a music lineup that includes R&B, hip-hop, and electronic hits, Peaches and

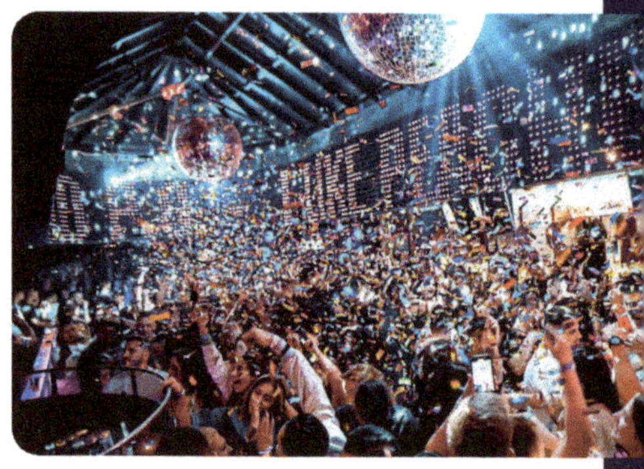

Cream attracts a vibrant crowd ready to dance the night away. The club is a top spot for those seeking a fun and dynamic nightlife experience. **Tip**: Arrive early or book a VIP table for a more comfortable experience. Keep an eye on their website for special events and themed nights.

Address: Nagymező u. 46-48, 1065 Budapest, Hungary
Website: www.peachesandcream.hu/en

A38

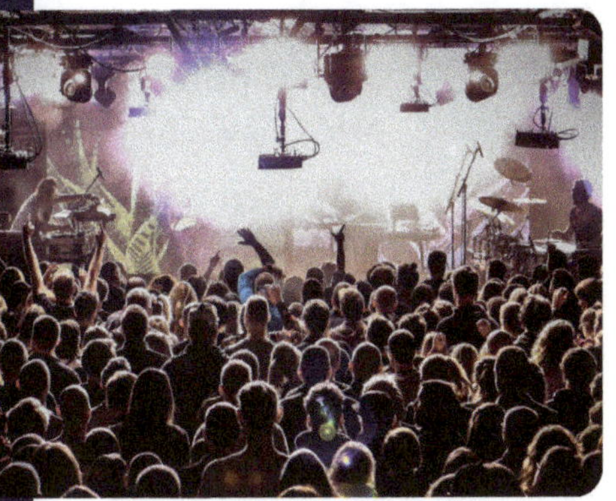

A38 is a unique nightclub and cultural venue located on a converted Ukrainian stone-carrier ship docked on the Danube River. Known for its eclectic mix of live music, DJ sets, and art exhibitions, A38 offers a diverse nightlife experience. The club features multiple stages and a rooftop terrace with stunning views of the city. A38 is celebrated for its cutting-edge performances and vibrant atmosphere.

Tip: Check the event schedule in advance to catch your favorite artists. Enjoy a drink on the rooftop terrace before heading to the main stage for an unforgettable night.

Address: Petőfi híd, Budai hídfő, 1117 Budapest, Hungary
Website: www.a38.hu/en

MORRISON'S 2

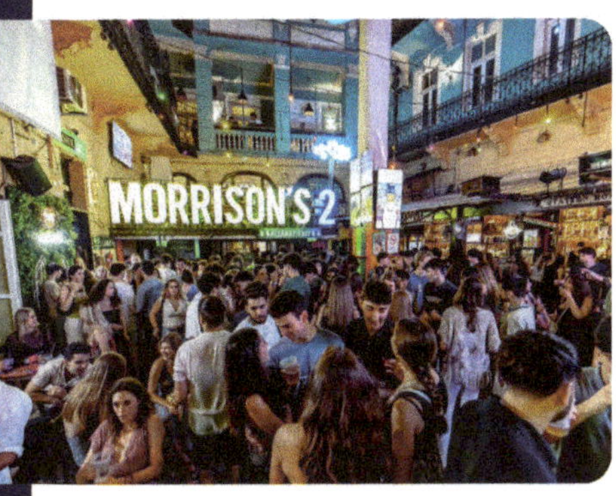

Morrison's 2 is a popular nightclub in Budapest, offering a lively atmosphere with multiple dance floors, karaoke rooms, and a spacious garden area. The club plays a variety of music genres, from retro hits to contemporary dance tracks, catering to a diverse crowd. Known for its affordable drinks and vibrant ambiance, Morrison's 2 is a great spot for a fun night out with friends.

Tip: Arrive early to take advantage of happy hour deals. Check their website for theme nights and special events to enhance your clubbing experience.

Address: Szent István krt. 11, 1055 Budapest, Hungary
Website: www.morrisons2.hu/en/

KARAVÁN STREET FOOD

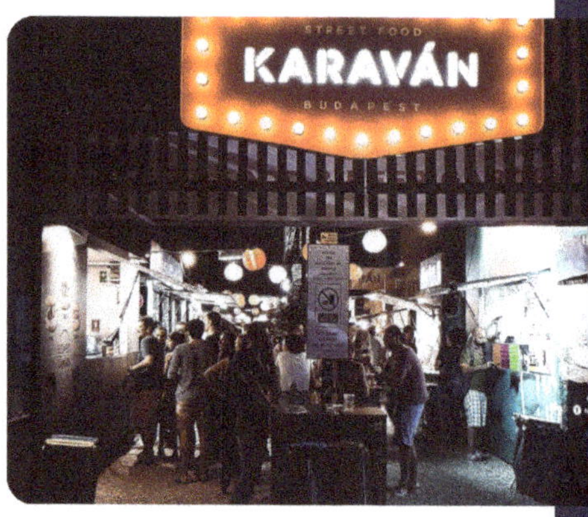

Karaván Street Food is a bustling open-air food court in Budapest's Jewish Quarter, offering a diverse array of local and international street food options. From traditional Hungarian dishes like lángos and goulash to vegan and gourmet burgers, Karaván caters to all tastes. The lively atmosphere and late-night hours make it a perfect spot for a quick bite after an evening out.

Tip: Try the lángos for an authentic Hungarian experience. Arrive with friends to sample multiple dishes from different vendors and enjoy the vibrant nightlife ambiance.

Address: Kazinczy u. 18, 1075 Budapest, Hungary
Website: www.facebook.com/streetfoodkaravan/

SPÍLER SHANGHAI

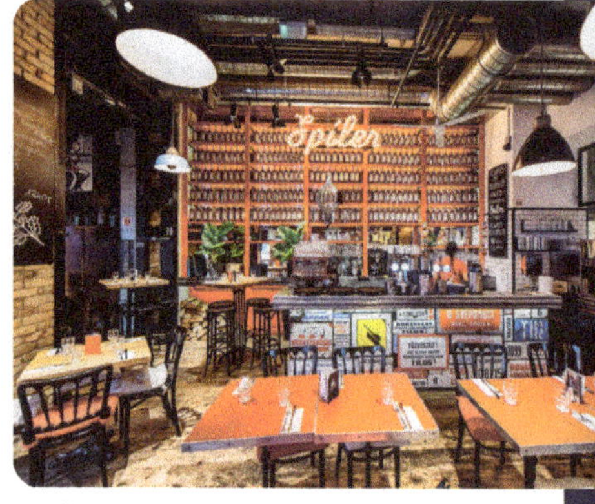

Spíler Shanghai, located in the bustling Gozsdu Udvar, offers a unique blend of Asian cuisine and contemporary flair. This stylish late-night eatery serves a variety of dishes, including dim sum, sushi, and wok specialties. The eclectic decor and energetic vibe make it a popular spot for late-night dining and socializing.

Tip: Visit during late-night hours for a more relaxed dining experience. Try their signature cocktails to complement the flavorful dishes. Make a reservation if you plan to visit on weekends,

as it gets quite busy.
Address: Király u. 13, 1075 Budapest, Hungary
Website: www.spilershanghai.hu/main-page.html

MAZEL TOV

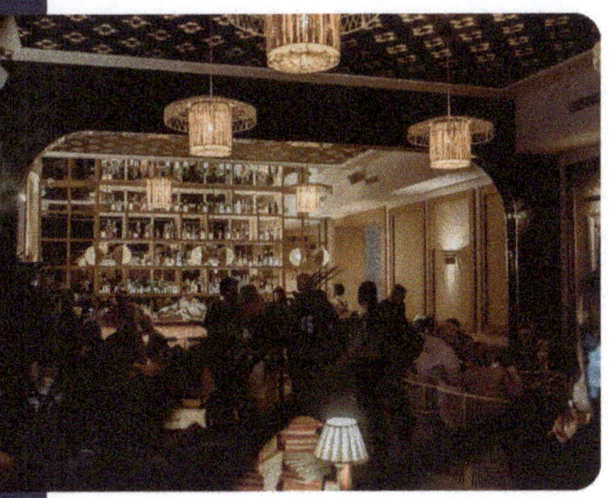

Mazel Tov is a vibrant ruin bar and restaurant in Budapest's Jewish Quarter, offering a delightful blend of Middle Eastern cuisine and lively ambiance. The beautifully decorated courtyard provides a cozy setting for enjoying dishes like shakshuka, hummus, and falafel. Open late, Mazel Tov is perfect for a relaxing meal after exploring the city's nightlife. **Tip**: Make a reservation to secure a table, especially on weekends. Don't miss their craft cocktails, which pair perfectly with the flavorful dishes.

Address: Akácfa u. 47, 1072 Budapest, Hungary
Website: www.mazeltov.hu/en

TRÓFEA GRILL RESTAURANT

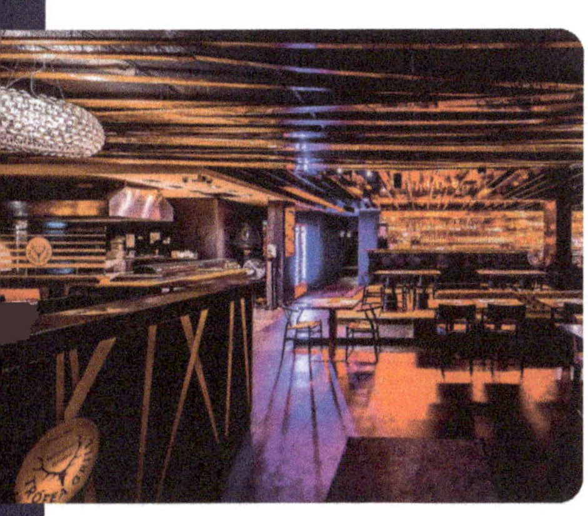

Trófea Grill Restaurant is a popular all-you-can-eat buffet that offers a wide range of Hungarian and international dishes. With its extensive menu, you can enjoy everything from traditional goulash to fresh salads and desserts. Open until late, Trófea Grill is ideal for satisfying late-night cravings in a welcoming environment.
Tip: Arrive with a hearty appetite to make the most of the buffet. Consider visiting during their late-night hours for a quieter dining experience and enjoy the diverse culinary offerings.

Address: Budapest, Király u. 30-32, 1061 Hungary
Website: www.trofea.hu/en

JEWISH QUARTER

Budapest's Jewish Quarter is a vibrant nightlife area known for its historic charm and bustling bar scene. This district is home to some of the city's most famous ruin pubs, including Szimpla Kert, and offers a unique blend of cultural heritage and modern entertainment. The narrow streets are lined with eclectic

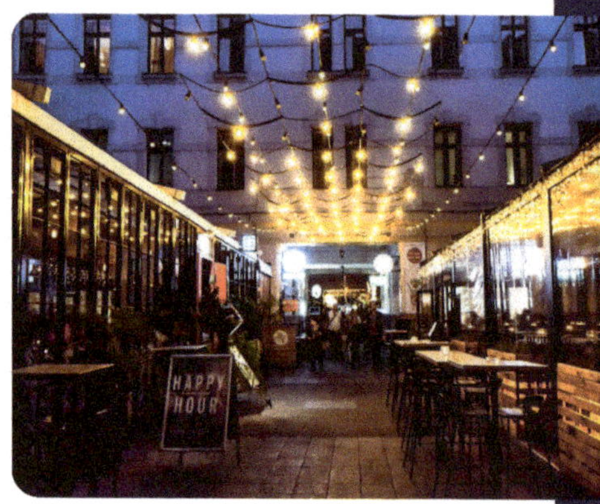

bars, trendy cafés, and late-night eateries, making it a hotspot for both locals and tourists. The area also features significant landmarks like the Dohány Street Synagogue.

Tip: Explore the area on foot to fully experience its lively atmosphere. Start your evening with a visit to a ruin pub and then enjoy some local street food at Karaván Street Food.

Address: District VII, Budapest, Hungary

ANDRÁSSY AVENUE

Andrássy Avenue, a UNESCO World Heritage site, transforms into a vibrant nightlife area as the sun sets. This elegant boulevard, known for its upscale boutiques and historic buildings, also houses several chic bars, sophisticated lounges, and trendy clubs. Visitors can enjoy a stylish evening out, sipping cocktails in glamorous

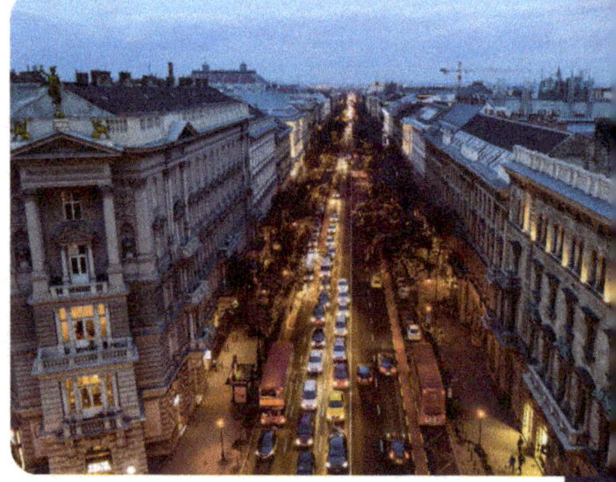

settings or dancing the night away in exclusive clubs. The avenue's beautiful architecture and lively atmosphere make it a perfect spot for a memorable night.

Tip: Start your evening with a visit to a rooftop bar for stunning views, then explore the clubs and lounges along the avenue for a complete nightlife experience.

Address: Andrássy út, 1061 Budapest, Hungary

Image credit: welovebudapest.com

RÁDAY STREET

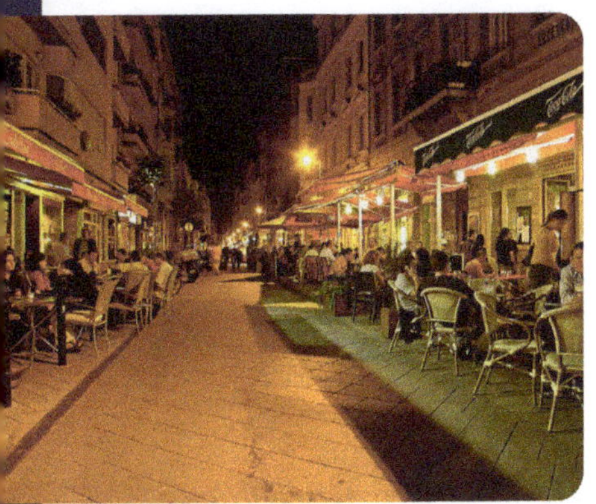

Ráday Street is a lively and vibrant nightlife area in Budapest, known for its diverse selection of bars, cafés, and restaurants. Stretching from Kálvin Square to Boráros Square, this pedestrian-friendly street is a hotspot for locals and tourists alike. It offers a mix of traditional Hungarian eateries, trendy bars, and international cuisine, creating a dynamic atmosphere perfect for an evening out. The street is also famous for its cultural events and live music, adding to the vibrant nightlife scene.

Tip: Start your evening with dinner at one of the traditional Hungarian restaurants, then explore the bars and enjoy live music. Visit during a street festival to experience the area at its most vibrant.

Address: Ráday utca, 1092 Budapest, Hungary

CORVIN QUARTER

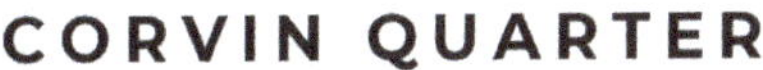

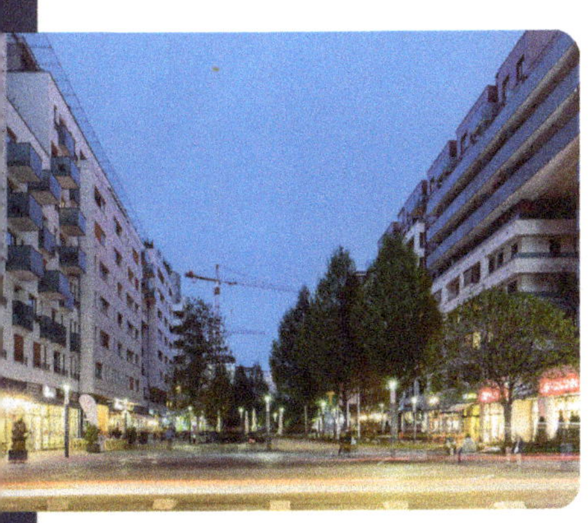

Corvin Quarter is an emerging nightlife district in Budapest, offering a mix of modern bars, pubs, and clubs. This area, centered around the Corvin Plaza, has become a hotspot for locals and tourists looking for a vibrant night out. The district features a variety of venues, from casual pubs with craft beers to stylish clubs with live DJs. Its lively and welcoming atmosphere makes it an excellent choice for a diverse and exciting evening.

Tip: Explore the different venues within the Corvin Plaza complex to find the perfect spot that suits your mood. Enjoy a meal at one of the nearby restaurants before diving into the nightlife.

Address: Corvin sétány, 1082 Budapest, Hungary

Exploring Budapest by night can be an exhilarating experience, but it's important to prioritize your safety to ensure your evening adventures remain pleasant memories. Here are some safety tips to keep in mind:

- **Vigilance is key**: Crowded venues and bustling streets are prime spots for pickpockets. Always be mindful of your personal belongings and consider using anti-theft bags or pouches.
- **Stay in the light**: Stick to well-lit and populated streets, especially if you're venturing out alone. Dark and deserted alleys can be risky, so it's best to avoid them.
- **Trustworthy transport**: Use only reputable taxi companies or verified ride-sharing apps for nighttime travel. It's wise to pre-save the contact details of a reliable taxi service on your phone.
- **Guard your glass**: While enjoying the local nightlife, never leave your drink unattended. Accept beverages only from trusted companions or directly from the bartender.
- **Drink smart**: Consume alcohol in moderation and stay hydrated with water throughout the night. This will help you maintain awareness and make better decisions.
- **Emergency preparedness**: Keep a list of emergency contacts, including local authorities and your embassy, easily accessible. A portable phone charger can be a lifesaver in keeping your device powered up.
- **Document safety**: Carry photocopies of your essential documents, such as your passport, and store the originals in a secure location like a hotel safe.

Remember, the night is yours to enjoy, but staying alert and prepared is the best way to ensure that your nocturnal explorations are safe and enjoyable.

By following these tips and exploring the city by night, you'll be able to experience the magic and charm of the city while staying safe and having an unforgettable time.

Budapest: A Confluence of Art, History, and Architecture

Budapest, affectionately known as the "Pearl of the Danube," stands as a grand testament to the layers of history, culture, and art that have shaped this vibrant city. Divided into Buda and Pest by the majestic Danube, Budapest presents a fascinating duality of medieval serenity and bustling cosmopolitan energy, linked by the storied Chain Bridge.

Artistically, Budapest is a canvas of historical richness and modern vitality. The city's art scene is punctuated by key institutions like the Hungarian National Gallery, which resides in the regal Buda Castle, showcasing a timeline of Hungarian art from medieval stone carvings to contemporary pieces. In Pest, the Museum of Fine Arts houses an impressive collection of international art, including works by European masters, underscoring Budapest's integral role in the pan-European art narrative.

The history of Budapest is as dynamic as its skyline. Originating from Roman times as Aquincum, the city has been the focal point of several major empires, including the Ottoman and the Austro-Hungarian. Each era has left indelible marks on the city's cultural and architectural heritage, from the ancient Roman ruins in Óbuda to the grandeur of the Austro-Hungarian architecture along Andrássy Avenue.

Architecturally, Budapest is a treasure trove of styles, each telling stories of different epochs. The city's architecture is a blend of everything from Baroque and Classicist to Art Nouveau and Bauhaus, with notable examples like the ornate State Opera House and the innovative design of the Széchenyi Thermal Bath. Moreover, Budapest's skyline is crowned by the Gothic Revival spire of the Parliament Building, one of the largest and most iconic legislative buildings in the world, illustrating the city's historic ties to Gothic architectural traditions.

Budapest, with its rich tapestry of art, history, and architecture, offers a multidimensional journey through time. It stands not just as a city, but as a living museum and a vibrant center for continuous cultural dialogue and artistic expression. For those drawn to the confluence of past and present, Budapest offers an enriching exploration of heritage and innovation.

ART AND CULTURE IN BUDAPEST

HUNGARIAN NATIONAL MUSEUM

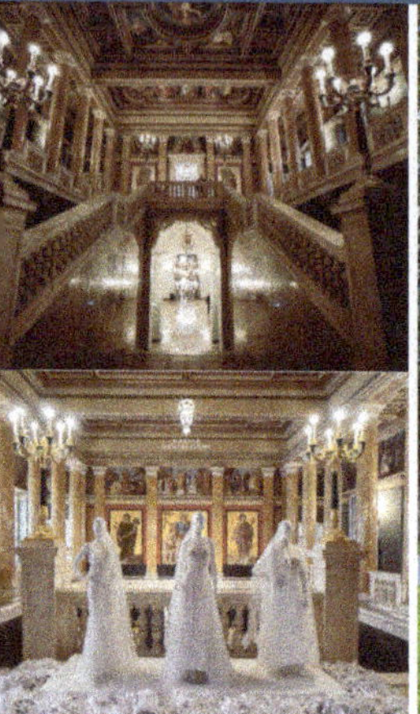

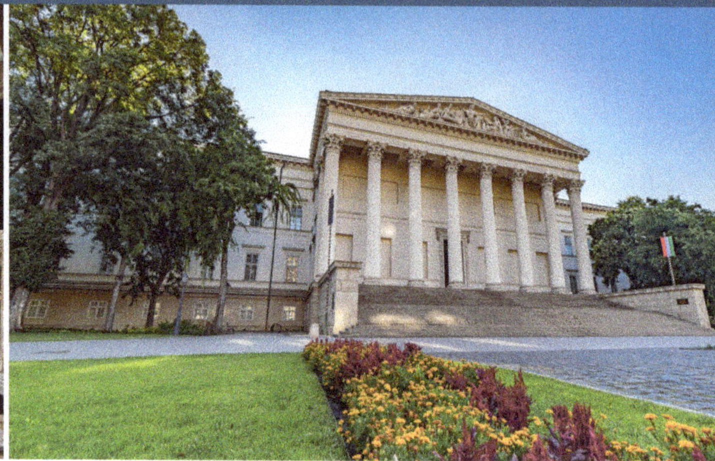

The Hungarian National Museum, established in 1802, is a cornerstone of Hungary's cultural heritage, offering a comprehensive look into the nation's history and art. Housed in a grand neoclassical building designed by Mihály Pollack, the museum's architecture is as impressive as its collections. Visitors can explore permanent exhibitions that span from prehistoric times to the modern era, including archaeological artifacts, medieval treasures, and relics from the Ottoman occupation.

One of the museum's highlights is the Coronation Mantle, a symbol of Hungary's royal history. The museum also showcases a variety of temporary exhibitions, educational programs, and cultural events, making it a vibrant center for learning and exploration. The beautifully landscaped garden surrounding the museum is a serene spot for a leisurely stroll, offering a peaceful escape from the bustling city.

Tip: Allocate at least a few hours to fully appreciate the extensive collections and exhibitions. Consider taking a guided tour for deeper insights into Hungary's rich history and cultural heritage. After your visit, relax in the museum's garden or visit one of the nearby cafés for a coffee. The museum is centrally located, making it a convenient stop while exploring Budapest's historic district.

Address: Múzeum krt. 14-16, 1088 Budapest, Hungary
Website: www.mnm.hu/en

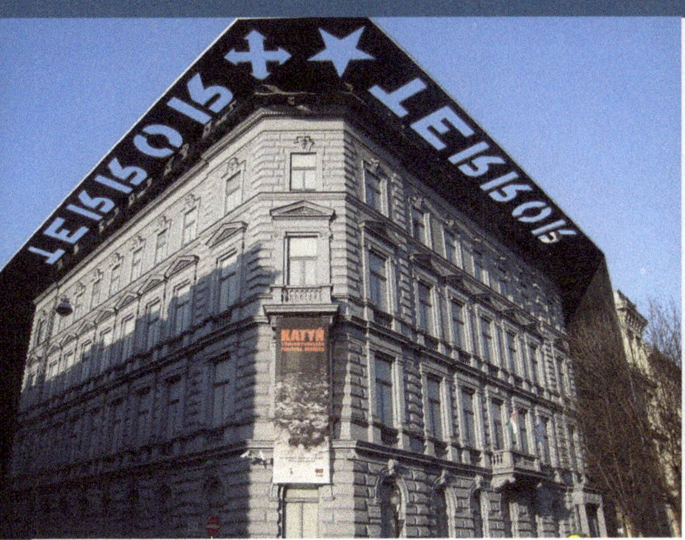

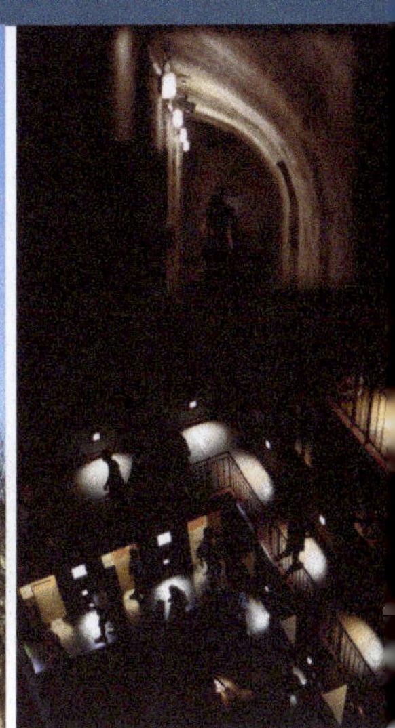

The House of Terror Museum is a poignant and powerful institution that chronicles Hungary's turbulent 20th-century history under fascist and communist regimes. Located in the former headquarters of the Arrow Cross Party and later the State Security services, the museum provides a sobering exploration of the oppressive forces that shaped Hungary's past. The building itself, with its stark exterior and dramatic "TERROR" signage, sets the tone for the emotional journey inside.

Visitors can explore meticulously curated exhibitions that include personal testimonies, photographs, and artifacts that depict the brutality and resilience of the Hungarian people. The basement, once used as a prison, gives a harrowing glimpse into the grim realities of political persecution and torture. Interactive displays and multimedia elements further enhance the museum's impact, making it an immersive educational experience.

Tip: Plan to spend at least two hours to fully engage with the exhibits and understand the context of Hungary's historical struggles. It's advisable to use the audio guide for detailed explanations. Due to the intense subject matter, the museum may not be suitable for young children. After visiting, take some time to reflect in the nearby City Park (Városliget) to decompress and process the museum's profound narratives.

Address: Andrássy út 60, 1062 Budapest, Hungary
Website: www.terrorhaza.hu/en/

LUDWIG MUSEUM OF CONTEMPORARY ART

The Ludwig Museum of Contemporary Art is a premier institution showcasing Hungarian and international contemporary art. Located in the modern Palace of Arts, the museum features rotating exhibitions and a permanent collection that includes works by renowned artists such as Andy Warhol and Roy Lichtenstein.

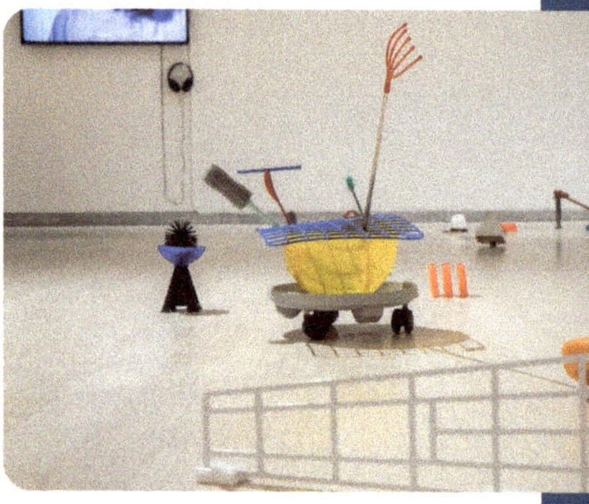

The diverse and dynamic exhibits offer a deep dive into contemporary artistic expressions.

Tip: Check the museum's schedule for special exhibitions and

events. Enjoy a coffee at the museum café, which offers beautiful views of the Danube River.
Address: Komor Marcell u. 1, 1095 Budapest, Hungary
Website: www.ludwigmuseum.hu/en

BUDAPEST HISTORY MUSEUM

The Budapest History Museum, located in Buda Castle, offers a rich exploration of the city's past from prehistoric times to the modern era. The museum's exhibits include medieval artifacts, Gothic sculptures, and interactive displays that vividly illustrate Budapest's historical development. Visitors can also tour reconstructed medieval

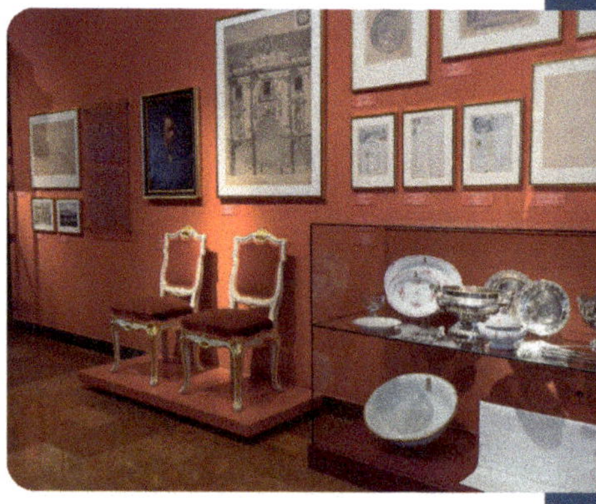

palace rooms, providing a glimpse into the grandeur of royal life.
Tip: Allocate a few hours for a thorough visit and combine it with a tour of Buda Castle for a complete historical experience.

Address: Szent György tér 2, 1014 Budapest, Hungary
Website: www.varmuzeum.hu

MUSEUM OF FINE ARTS

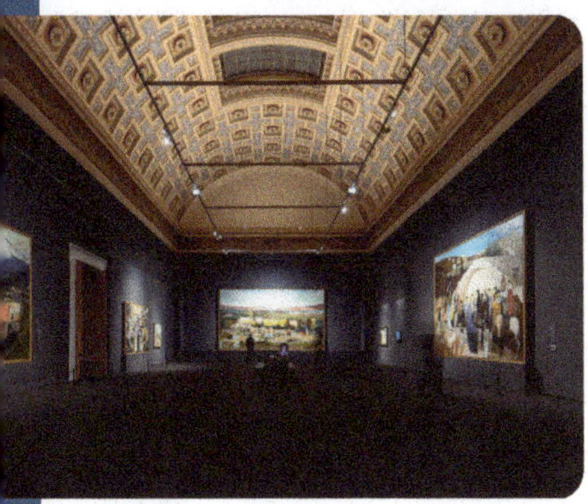

The Museum of Fine Arts in Budapest houses an extensive collection of European art from ancient times to the present day. Located in Heroes' Square, this grand museum features works by masters such as Raphael, El Greco, and Rembrandt, alongside Egyptian antiquities and classical sculptures. The recently renovated museum offers an impressive journey through art history.

Tip: Allocate extra time for the special exhibitions and visit the nearby Heroes' Square and City Park for a full cultural day out.

Address: Dózsa György út 41, 1146 Budapest, Hungary
Website: www.mfab.hu

LISZT FERENC MUSIC ACADEMY

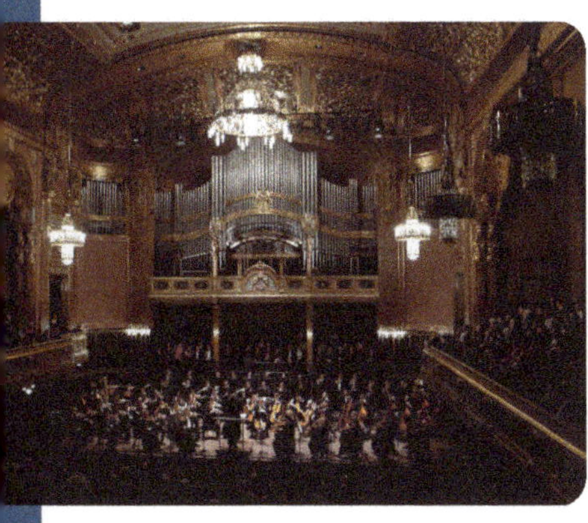

The Liszt Ferenc Music Academy, named after the famous Hungarian composer Franz Liszt, is both a prestigious music conservatory and a concert hall. The stunning Art Nouveau building hosts a variety of classical music performances, showcasing the talents of students and renowned musicians alike. The academy is a cultural gem in Budapest's music scene.

Tip: Attend a concert to experience the exceptional acoustics and musical talent. Take a guided tour to learn about the academy's history and architecture.

Address: Liszt Ferenc tér 8, 1061 Budapest, Hungary
Website: https://uni.lisztacademy.hu/

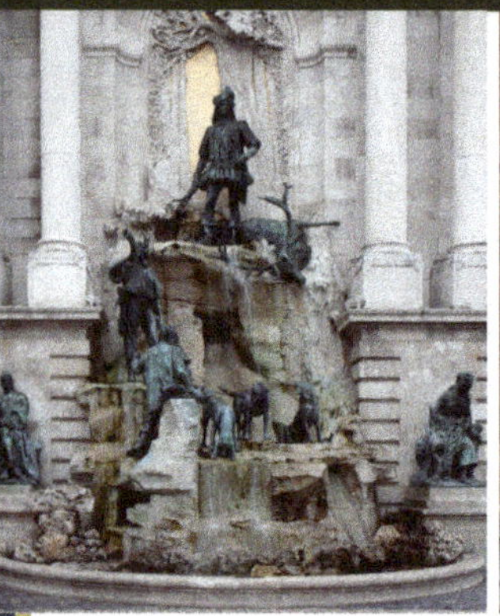
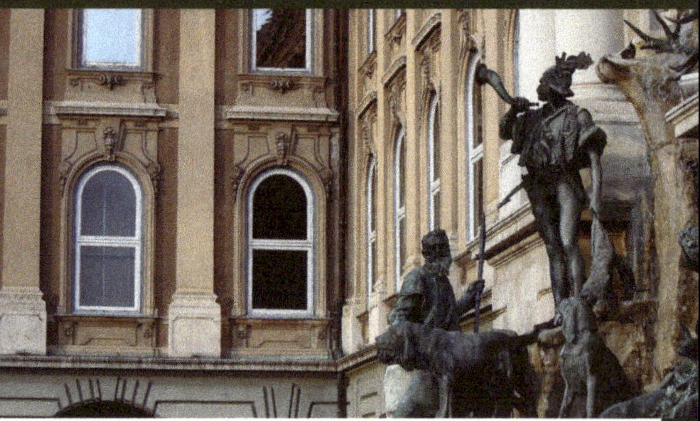

Matthias Fountain, located in the western courtyard of Buda Castle, is an iconic Baroque-style fountain and one of Budapest's most beloved landmarks. Created by sculptor Alajos Stróbl in 1904, the fountain presents a dynamic and lifelike hunting scene featuring King Matthias Corvinus. The sculpture captures the king and his hunting party, including a beautiful maiden, hunting dogs, and a slain deer, all arranged in a strikingly detailed composition. The cascading water adds a sense of movement and life to the scene, making it a captivating sight for visitors.

The fountain's intricate details and the surrounding historical setting of Buda Castle make it a must-visit attraction. The statue of the king, standing proudly above the group, symbolizes his revered status in Hungarian history. The accompanying figures and animals are meticulously crafted, showcasing the high artistic standards of the time.

Tip: Visit Matthias Fountain in the late afternoon when the sunlight casts a warm glow on the sculpture, highlighting its intricate details. After admiring the fountain, take time to explore the surrounding Buda Castle area for more historical attractions and panoramic views of Budapest. The castle grounds offer a perfect blend of history, architecture, and scenic beauty, ensuring a memorable experience.

Address: Buda Castle, Szent György tér 2, 1014 Budapest,

Website: www.budacastlebudapest.com/matthias-fountain-buda-castle-district/

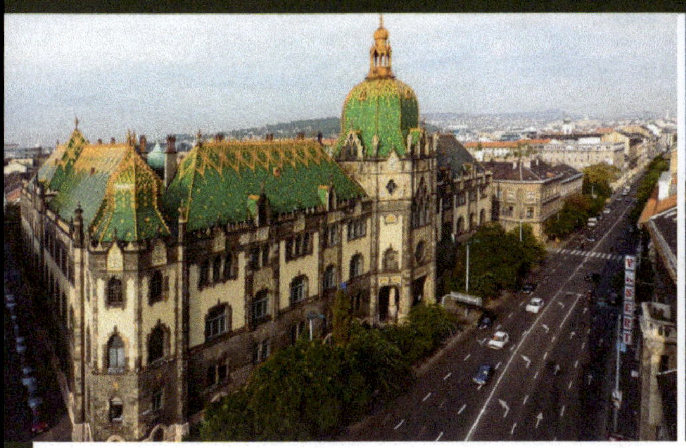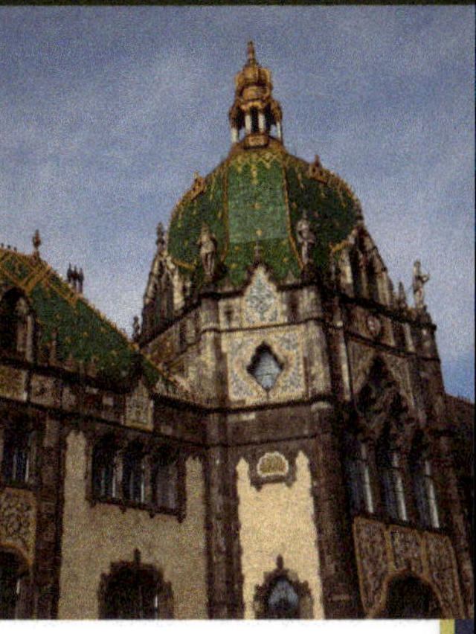

The Museum of Applied Arts in Budapest is a stunning architectural and cultural landmark that showcases a vast collection of decorative arts and design. Founded in 1872, the museum is housed in an exquisite building designed by the renowned architect Ödön Lechner, often referred to as the "Hungarian Gaudí." The building itself is a masterpiece of Art Nouveau architecture, featuring a striking green Zsolnay ceramic roof and intricate ornamental details that blend Hungarian folk motifs with Eastern influences.

Inside, the museum's diverse collection spans centuries and includes furniture, textiles, ceramics, glassware, and metalwork from Hungary and beyond. The exhibitions highlight the evolution of applied arts and design, offering visitors a glimpse into the craftsmanship and creativity that define these disciplines. Temporary exhibitions and special events further enrich the museum experience, making it a dynamic center for art and culture.

The museum's beautiful interior, with its grand hall and elegant staircases, enhances the visitor experience, providing a fitting backdrop for the displayed artifacts. The Museum of Applied Arts is not only a treasure trove of decorative arts but also an architectural gem that reflects Hungary's rich cultural heritage.

Tip: Allocate extra time to appreciate the building's architecture both inside and out. Check the museum's schedule for temporary exhibitions and events. After your visit, explore the nearby Great Market Hall for a taste of local culture and cuisine.

Address: Üllői út 33-37, 1091 Budapest, Hungary
Website: www.imm.hu/en/

RUDAS BATHS

Rudas Baths, a historical thermal bathhouse, dates back to the 16th-century Ottoman era. Known for its beautiful Turkish architecture, the bathhouse features a central octagonal pool, smaller thermal pools, and a modern wellness area. The rooftop pool offers stunning views of the Danube and the city skyline, making it a

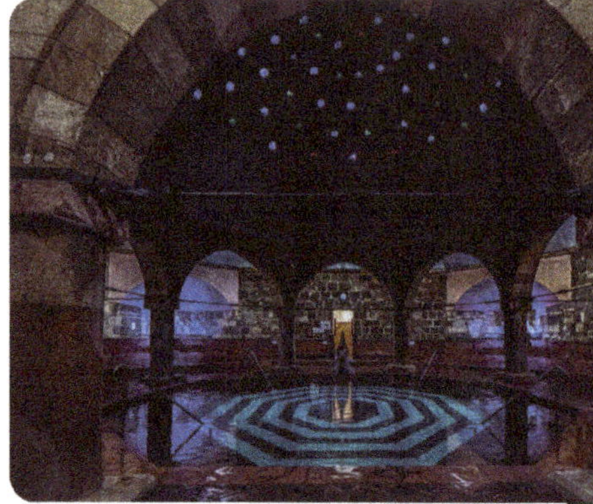

unique place to relax and soak in Budapest's rich history.
Tip: Visit during the evening for a tranquil experience and enjoy the illuminated city views from the rooftop pool.

Address: Döbrentei tér 9, 1013 Budapest, Hungary
Website: https://en.rudasfurdo.hu/

ST. MARGARET'S CHURCH RUINS

The St. Margaret's Church Ruins, located on Margaret Island, are the remnants of a 13th-century Dominican church. Named after St. Margaret of Hungary, who lived and died here, the site offers a peaceful retreat and a glimpse into medieval religious life. The ruins are surrounded by beautiful gardens, making it a serene

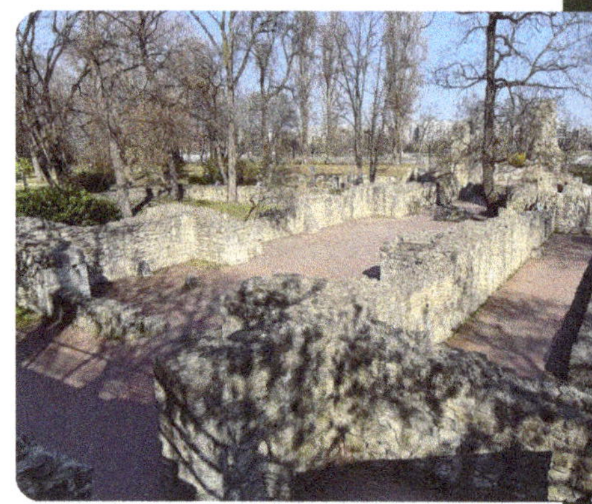

spot for contemplation and exploration.
Tip: Combine your visit with a leisurely stroll around Margaret Island's parks and gardens.

Address: Margaret Island, 1138 Budapest, Hungary
Website: www.budapestinfo.hu/en/margaret-island-1

BUDA TOWER (MARY MAGDALENE TOWER)

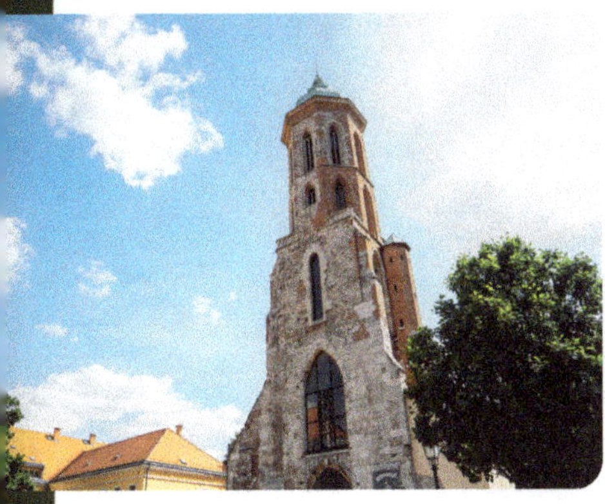

The Buda Tower, also known as Mary Magdalene Tower, is a historical landmark representing the remnants of a 13th-century Gothic church. Initially serving as a parish church, it was later converted to a mosque during the Ottoman occupation. The tower offers panoramic views of the Buda Castle District and the surrounding city, making it a must-visit for history enthusiasts and photographers.

Tip: Climb to the top of the tower for stunning views. Visit in the late afternoon for the best light for photography and to avoid the midday crowds.

Address: Kapisztrán tér 6, 1014 Budapest, Hungary
Website: www.budatower.hu/en/

UNIVERSITY CHURCH

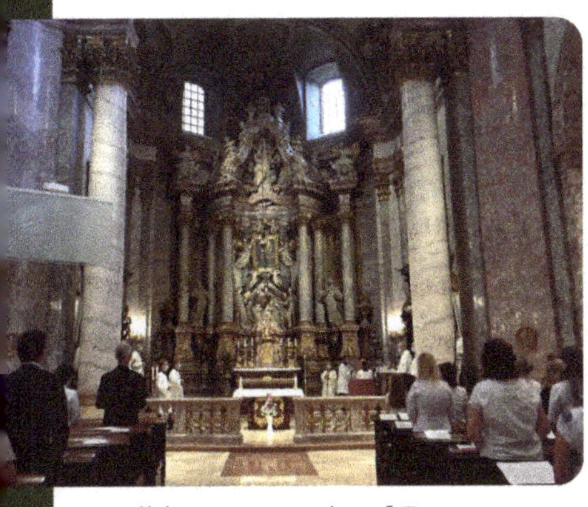

The University Church, also known as the Church of the Blessed Virgin Mary the Queen, is a Baroque masterpiece located in the heart of Budapest. Built in the 18th century, the church features stunning frescoes, intricate woodwork, and a richly decorated interior. The facade, with its twin towers and elaborate sculptures, is a striking example of Baroque architecture.

Tip: Attend a service to experience the church's acoustic beauty. Explore the surrounding area, which is filled with quaint cafés and shops, for a complete cultural experience.

Address: Papnövelde u. 8, 1053 Budapest, Hungary
Website: www.egyetemitemplom.com

DAY TRIPS FROM BUDAPEST
SZENTENDRE

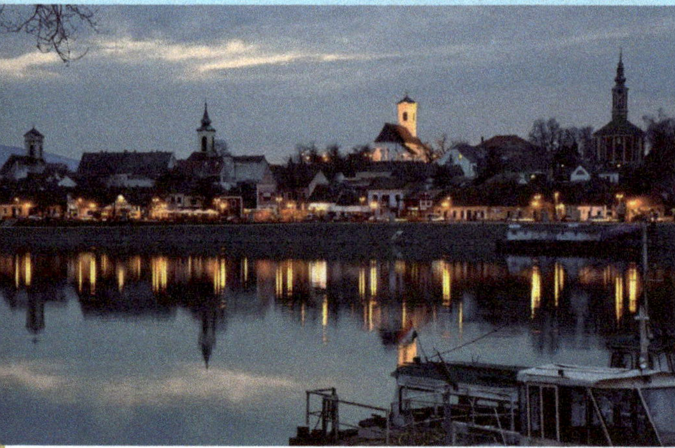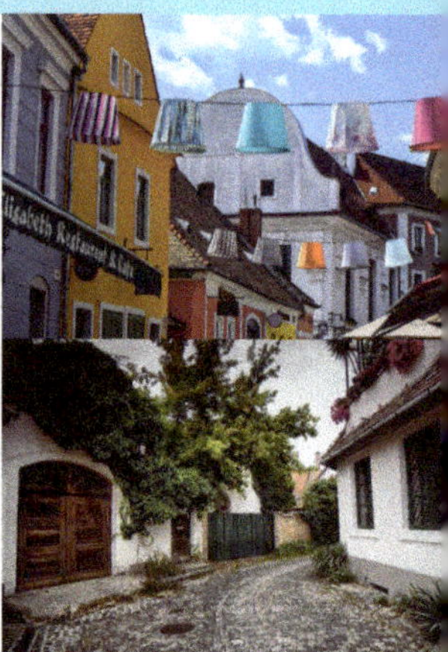

Szentendre, located just 20 kilometers north of Budapest, is a charming riverside town renowned for its vibrant art scene and picturesque streets. A short 40-minute train ride from Budapest's Batthyány Square transports visitors to this delightful destination. Szentendre boasts a rich cultural heritage with numerous museums, galleries, and churches reflecting its diverse history. The town's cobblestone streets and colorful Baroque houses create a unique and inviting atmosphere.

Upon arrival, visitors can explore the Szentendre Art Mill, the Marzipan Museum, and various art galleries showcasing contemporary and traditional Hungarian art. The main square, Fő tér, is a bustling hub with charming cafés and shops offering local crafts and souvenirs. The serene riverside promenade is perfect for a leisurely stroll or a relaxing afternoon by the Danube.

Getting There: Take the HÉV suburban train from Batthyány Square in Budapest.

Tip: Visit the town on a weekday to avoid the weekend crowds. Don't miss the open-air Skanzen Village Museum, which offers a fascinating insight into traditional Hungarian rural life. Many shops and galleries offer local crafts and artworks, making it a perfect place to pick up unique souvenirs.

Location: Szentendre, Hungary
Website: www.iranyszentendre.hu/en/

Visegrád, located just 40 kilometers north of Budapest, is a historic town renowned for its medieval heritage and stunning natural beauty. A scenic one-hour drive or a relaxing boat trip along the Danube River brings visitors to this picturesque destination. Visegrád offers a wealth of attractions, including the impressive Visegrád Castle, which sits atop a hill and provides breathtaking views of the Danube Bend.

The town's highlights include the Royal Palace, where visitors can explore the remains of the Renaissance palace of King Matthias Corvinus. The Solomon Tower, part of the town's ancient fortifications, offers a glimpse into Visegrád's medieval past. For those seeking outdoor activities, the surrounding hills provide excellent hiking trails with panoramic vistas.

Nature enthusiasts will appreciate the nearby Pilis Mountains and the panoramic views from the top of Castle Hill. The Danube-Ipoly National Park, which surrounds Visegrád, offers numerous outdoor activities such as hiking, biking, and bird-watching, making it a perfect destination for adventure seekers.

Getting There: Take a boat from Budapest's Vigadó Square or drive via Route 11.

Tip: Visit the castle in the early morning or late afternoon to avoid crowds and enjoy the best views. Don't miss the annual International Palace Games in July, where the town transforms into a medieval festival with jousting, archery, and traditional crafts.

Location: Visegrád, Hungary
Website: www.visegradturizam.com/en/home/

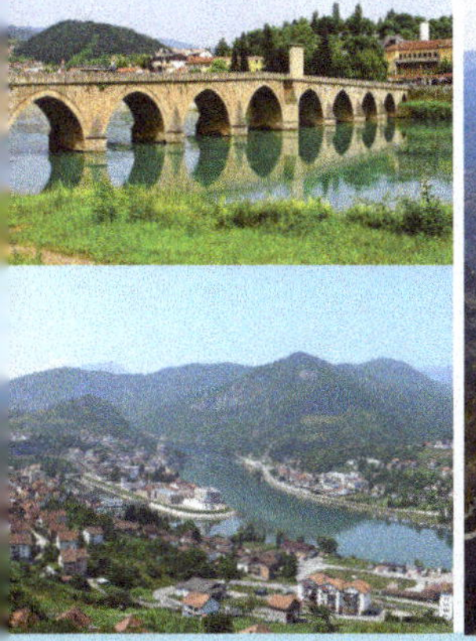

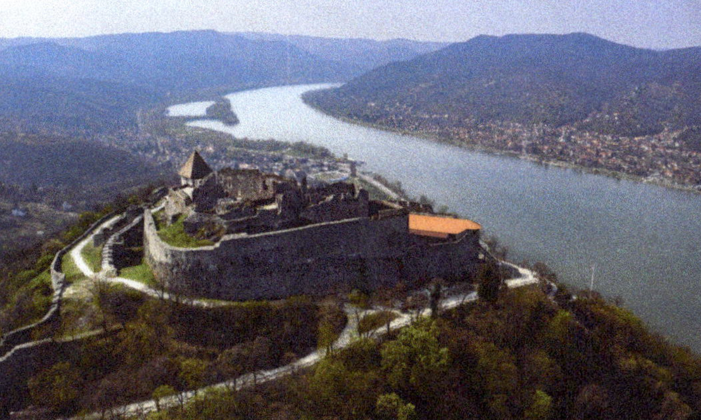

GÖDÖLLŐ PALACE

Gödöllő Palace, located just 30 kilometers northeast of Budapest, is one of Hungary's most magnificent baroque palaces. A short 30-minute train ride from Budapest's Keleti Railway Station transports visitors to this opulent royal residence. The palace, originally built in the 18th century, served as the summer residence for Queen Elisabeth (Sisi) and Emperor Franz Joseph. It offers a fascinating glimpse into the life and times of the Habsburg monarchy.

The palace boasts beautifully restored rooms, exquisite frescoes, and a grand ballroom. Visitors can explore the royal apartments, the ceremonial hall, and the palace chapel. The extensive landscaped gardens and park surrounding the palace are perfect for leisurely strolls, providing a tranquil escape from the bustle of Budapest. Seasonal exhibitions and events further enrich the visitor experience, showcasing the palace's cultural and historical significance.

Getting There: Take a train from Budapest's Keleti Railway Station to Gödöllő.

Tip: Visit the palace during spring or summer when the gardens are in full bloom. Consider taking a guided tour to gain deeper insights into the history of the palace and the Habsburgs. Don't miss the palace café for a delightful break with views of the beautiful grounds.

Location: Gödöllő, Hungary
Website: www.kiralyikastely.hu/royal-palace-of-godollo.html

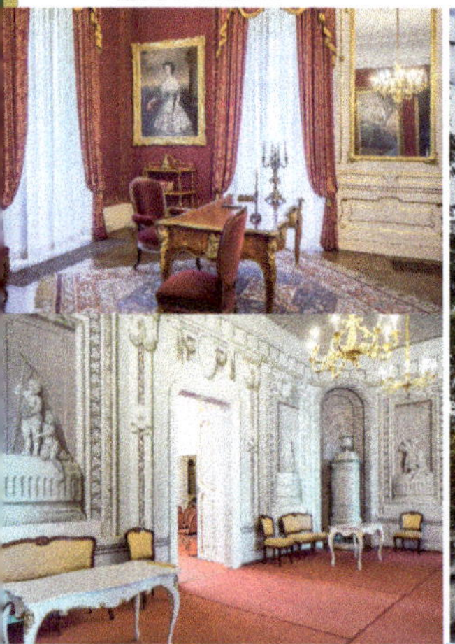

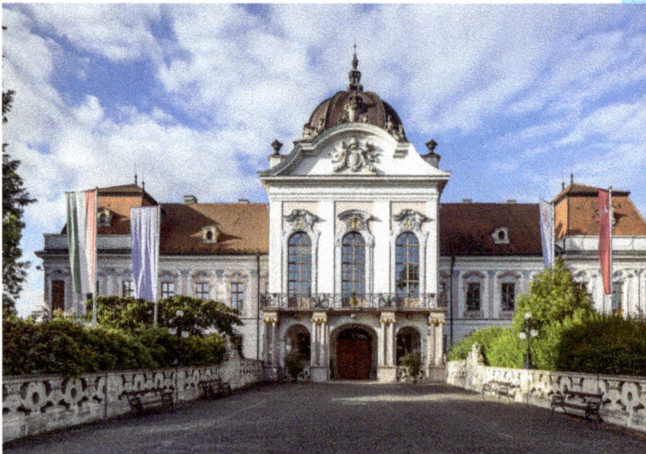

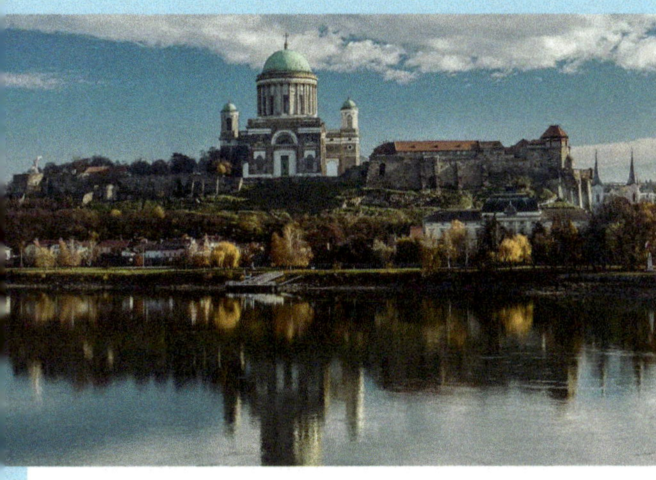
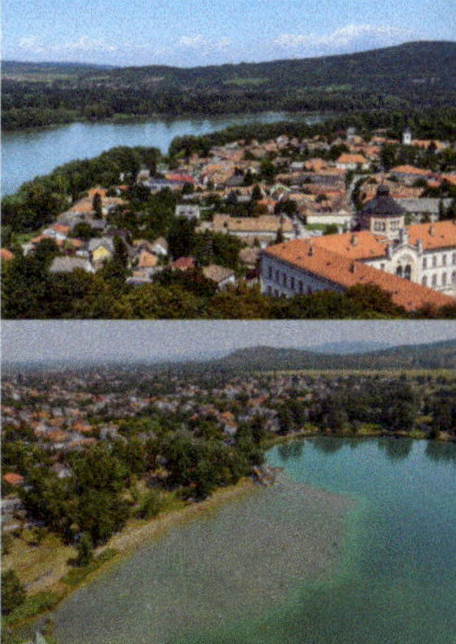

Esztergom, located just 46 kilometers north of Budapest, is a historic town known as the birthplace of Hungarian Christianity. A short one-hour train ride from Budapest's Nyugati Railway Station brings visitors to this significant cultural destination. Esztergom is home to the grand Esztergom Basilica, the largest church in Hungary and a masterpiece of Neoclassical architecture. The basilica's impressive dome and ornate interior make it a must-visit site.

In addition to the basilica, visitors can explore the Christian Museum, which houses a vast collection of medieval and Renaissance art. The Danube River, which runs through Esztergom, provides picturesque views and opportunities for leisurely riverside walks. The town's rich history is further highlighted by the remains of the Royal Palace and the Castle Museum, offering insights into Hungary's medieval past.

Getting There: Take a train from Budapest's Nyugati Railway Station to Esztergom.

Tip: Climb to the top of the basilica's dome for breathtaking panoramic views of the Danube and the surrounding countryside. Visit on a weekday to avoid the weekend crowds and enjoy a more peaceful experience. After exploring, relax at one of the local cafés along the riverbank for a taste of Hungarian hospitality and scenic views.

Location: Esztergom, Hungary
Website: www.visitesztergom.hu/en/

Lake Balaton, located about 80 kilometers southwest of Budapest, is the largest freshwater lake in Central Europe and a popular destination for both relaxation and adventure. A short 90-minute train ride or drive from Budapest brings visitors to this scenic retreat. Known as the "Hungarian Sea," Lake Balaton offers a wide range of activities, from swimming and sailing to hiking and wine tasting.

The northern shore, with its rolling hills and vineyards, is perfect for those seeking picturesque landscapes and charming towns like Balatonfüred and Tihany. Balatonfüred is renowned for its historic spa culture and vibrant marina, while Tihany is famous for its Benedictine Abbey and lavender fields. The southern shore features sandy beaches and bustling resorts like Siófok, ideal for families and water sports enthusiasts.

Getting There: Take a train from Budapest's Déli Railway Station to various towns along the lake.

Tip: Visit in the summer for the best beach experience and water activities. For a more tranquil visit, consider exploring the lake's northern shore during the off-season. Don't miss the local wines from the Balaton wine region, especially the crisp whites and refreshing rosés. A boat tour on the lake offers spectacular views and a relaxing way to enjoy the natural beauty.

Location: Lake Balaton, Hungary
Website: www.turizmus.balatonfured.hu/en/

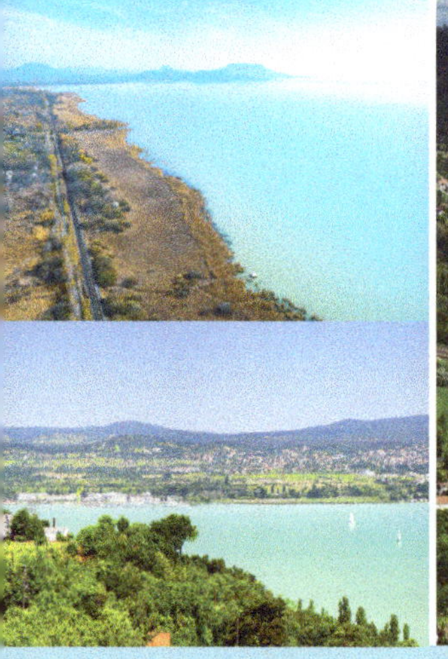

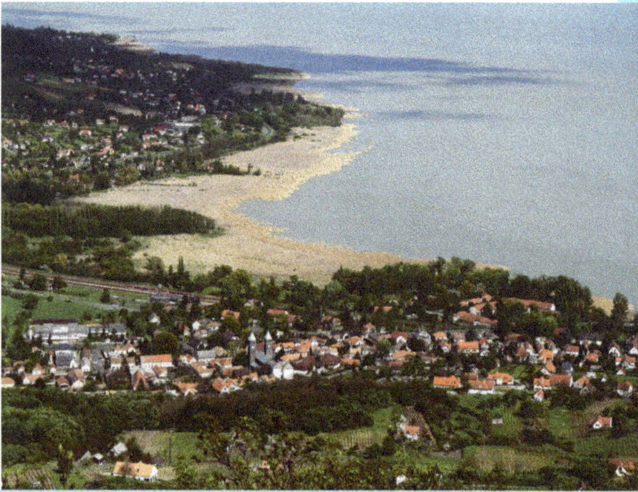

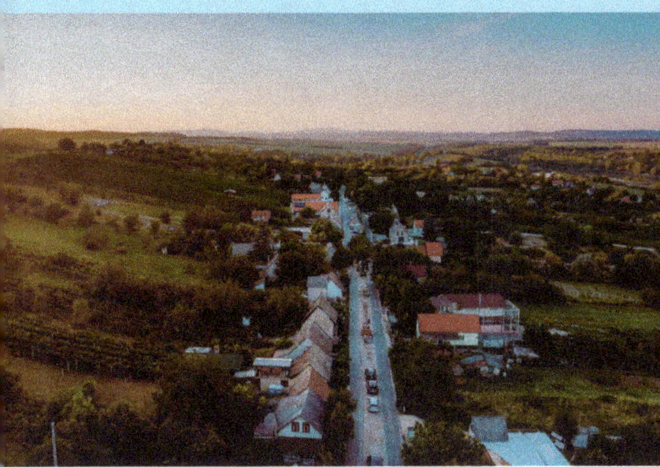
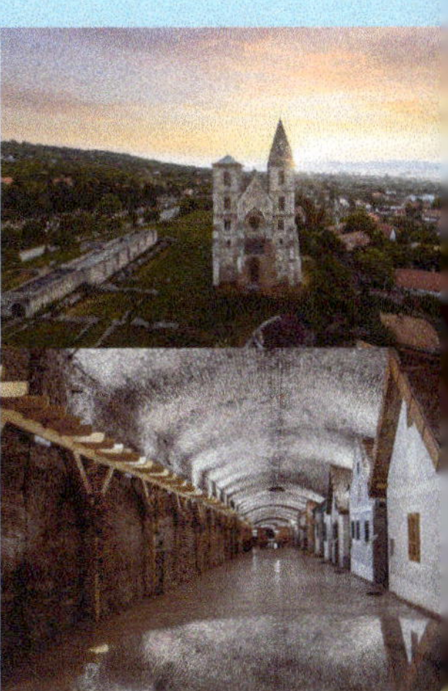

Etyek Wine Region, located just 30 kilometers west of Budapest, is renowned for its picturesque vineyards and exceptional wines. A short 30-minute drive from Budapest transports visitors to this charming region, often referred to as the "vineyard of Budapest." Etyek is celebrated for its crisp white wines and sparkling wines, offering a delightful experience for wine enthusiasts and casual visitors alike.

Visitors can tour numerous family-run wineries and larger estates, where they can learn about the winemaking process and sample a variety of local wines. The region's rolling hills and scenic landscapes provide a perfect backdrop for wine tasting and leisurely strolls. Etyek also hosts several wine festivals throughout the year, where visitors can enjoy live music, local cuisine, and, of course, excellent wine.

Getting There: Drive from Budapest or take a bus from Kelenföld Bus Station.

Tip: Visit during the spring or autumn to experience the wine region at its most beautiful. Join a guided wine tour to explore multiple wineries and gain insights into the local wine culture. Don't miss trying the region's sparkling wines, which are among the best in Hungary. For a complete experience, pair your wine tasting with a meal at one of the local restaurants, where you can enjoy traditional Hungarian dishes.

Location: Etyek, Hungary
Website: www.winesofhungary.hu/wine-tourism/etyek-buda-wine-district

HOLLÓKŐ

Hollókő, located just 100 kilometers northeast of Budapest, is a UNESCO World Heritage site known for its well-preserved traditional village and vibrant cultural heritage. A 90-minute drive from Budapest transports visitors to this charming rural destination, offering a glimpse into Hungary's past. The village features authentic 17th and 18th-century houses, a medieval castle, and beautiful landscapes.

Hollókő is renowned for its rich traditions and folklore, which are especially vibrant during the Easter Festival when locals dress in traditional costumes and celebrate with folk music, dance, and crafts. The village's open-air museum and various craft shops provide insights into traditional Hungarian village life. Visitors can also explore Hollókő Castle, which offers panoramic views of the surrounding hills and valleys.

Getting There: Drive from Budapest or take a bus from Puskás Ferenc Stadion bus station to Hollókő.

Tip: Visit during the Easter Festival to experience the village at its liveliest and most colorful. For a more tranquil visit, explore the nature trails around the village, which offer stunning views and peaceful settings. Don't forget to sample local delicacies at one of the village's traditional restaurants, where you can enjoy authentic Hungarian cuisine in a historic setting.

Location: Hollókő, Hungary
Website: www.holloko.hu

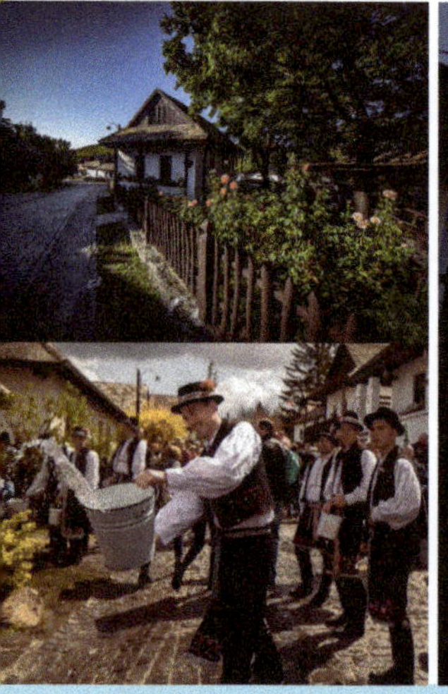

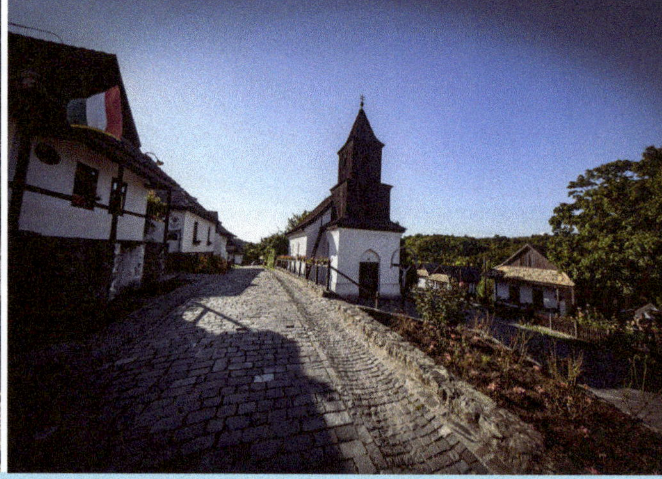

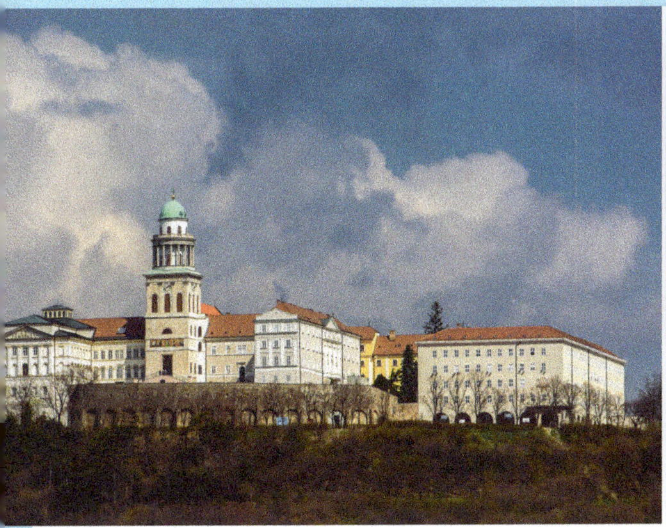

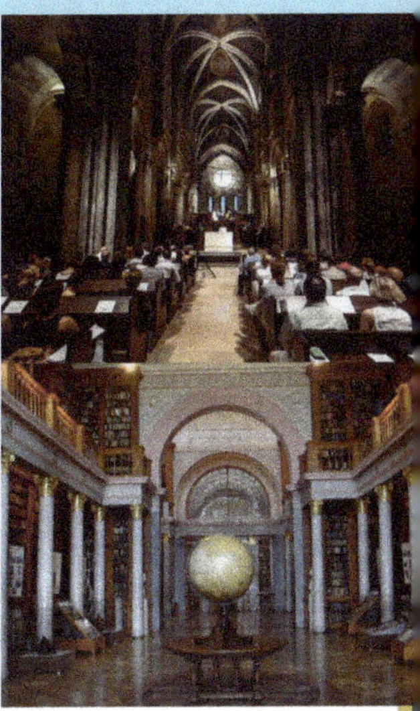

Pannonhalma Archabbey, located 120 kilometers northwest of Budapest, is one of Hungary's most significant historical and religious sites. Founded in 996, this Benedictine monastery is a UNESCO World Heritage site, known for its stunning architecture, rich history, and serene surroundings. A 90-minute drive from Budapest transports visitors to this spiritual and cultural haven.

Visitors can explore the impressive basilica, the beautiful cloisters, and the extensive library, which houses over 360,000 volumes, including many rare manuscripts. The abbey's arboretum and medicinal herb garden offer a peaceful retreat, perfect for a leisurely stroll. The on-site winery, run by the monks, produces acclaimed wines that visitors can sample and purchase.

Getting There: Drive from Budapest or take a train to Győr and then a short taxi ride to Pannonhalma.

Tip: Plan your visit to coincide with one of the guided tours to gain deeper insights into the abbey's history and daily life of the monks. Don't miss the opportunity to taste the monastery's own wines and herbal products. The abbey hosts various cultural events and concerts throughout the year, so check the schedule in advance to enhance your visit.

Location: 9090 Pannonhalma, Vár 1, Hungary
Website: https://foapatsagiturizmus.hu/

Tata, located approximately 70 kilometers west of Budapest, is a charming town known for its beautiful lakes, historic sites, and lush parks. A short one-hour drive or train ride from Budapest brings visitors to this serene destination. The town is renowned for its stunning Old Lake (Öreg-tó) and the picturesque Tata Castle, which dates back to the 14th century and is situated on the lake's edge.

Tata offers a range of outdoor activities, including boating, fishing, and hiking around its scenic lakes. The English Garden, a beautifully landscaped park, is perfect for leisurely strolls and picnics. Additionally, the town hosts several festivals throughout the year, such as the Water, Music, and Flower Festival, which celebrates the town's natural and cultural heritage.

Getting There: Drive from Budapest or take a train from Déli Railway Station to Tata.

Tip: Visit Tata Castle for a glimpse into the town's rich history and enjoy the panoramic views of Old Lake. Plan your visit during one of Tata's vibrant festivals for a unique cultural experience. For a relaxing afternoon, rent a boat on the lake or enjoy a meal at one of the lakeside restaurants, where you can savor local Hungarian cuisine while taking in the serene views.

Location: Tata, Hungary
Website: www.visittata.com

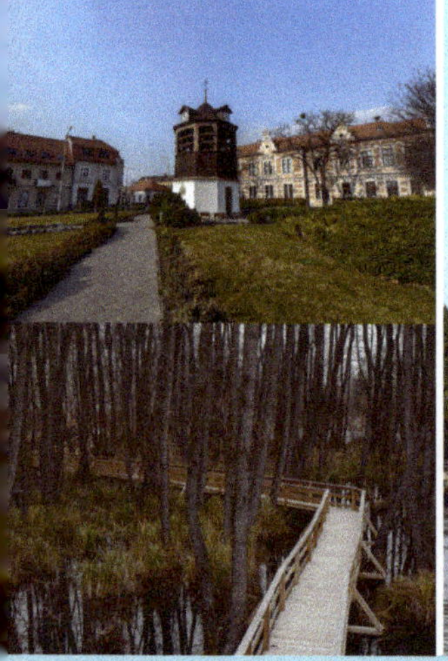

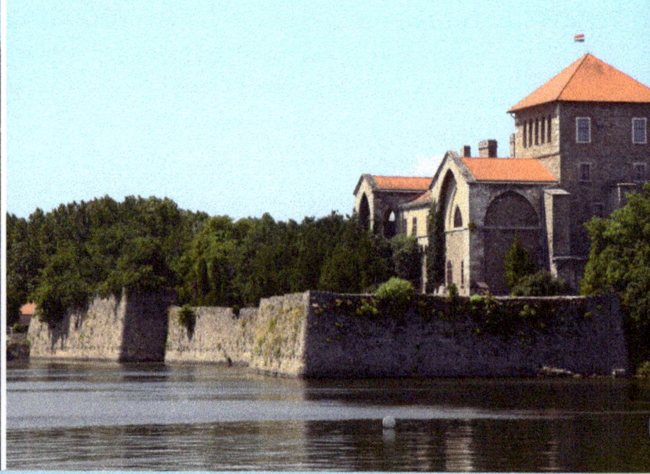

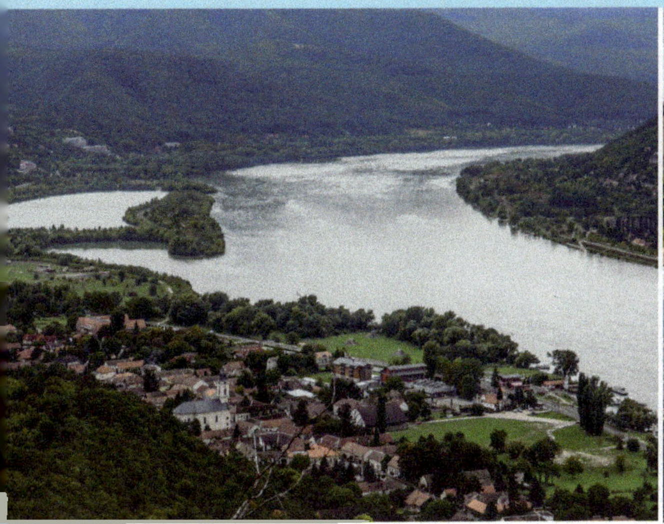

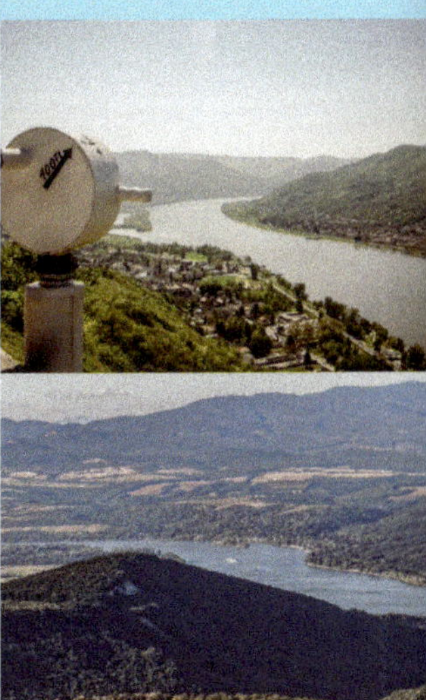

The Danube Bend, located just 50 kilometers north of Budapest, is a stunning natural region where the Danube River makes a dramatic turn, offering breathtaking views and rich cultural experiences. A short one-hour drive or train ride from Budapest brings visitors to this picturesque area, which includes the charming towns of Visegrád, Esztergom, and Szentendre.

The region is renowned for its scenic beauty, with opportunities for hiking, cycling, and river cruises. Visegrád offers historical attractions like the Visegrád Castle and Royal Palace, while Esztergom is home to Hungary's largest basilica. Szentendre, with its vibrant art scene and cobblestone streets, is perfect for leisurely strolls and exploring local galleries and museums.

Getting There: Drive from Budapest or take a train from Nyugati Railway Station to various towns along the Danube Bend.

Tip: For the best experience, take a river cruise to enjoy the stunning landscapes from the water. Visit in the spring or autumn for pleasant weather and fewer crowds. Each town in the Danube Bend offers unique attractions, so plan your trip to include visits to Visegrád, Esztergom, and Szentendre. Don't forget to bring your camera to capture the spectacular views and historic sites.

Location: Danube Bend, Hungary
Website: www.budapestinfo.hu/en/outings-around-budapest

END NOTE

As you conclude your journey through the vibrant city of Budapest, we hope this travel guide has enriched your understanding and appreciation of Hungary's captivating capital. From its majestic historical landmarks and architectural marvels to its lively cultural scene and serene natural escapes, Budapest offers an unforgettable experience for every traveler.

Budapest is a city where the past and present harmoniously coexist. The grandeur of its historical sites, such as Buda Castle, the Hungarian Parliament Building, and St. Stephen's Basilica, tells the story of a rich and tumultuous history. Walking through these landmarks, one can't help but feel connected to the countless generations that have shaped this city.

The culinary landscape of Budapest is another facet that will leave a lasting impression. Whether you are dining at a Michelin-starred restaurant like Onyx, savoring traditional Hungarian dishes at a local eatery, or exploring the bustling Great Market Hall, Budapest's food scene is as diverse as it is delicious. Don't miss the opportunity to try local favorites like goulash, kürtőskalács (chimney cake), and the famous Tokaji wine.

Budapest's unique charm is also evident in its natural beauty. The tranquil parks and gardens, such as Margaret Island and City Park, offer a peaceful retreat from the urban hustle. The thermal baths, including Széchenyi Thermal Bath and Rudas Baths, provide a rejuvenating experience that combines wellness with history.

As you venture beyond the city limits, day trips to places like Szentendre, Visegrád, and the Danube Bend reveal even more of Hungary's enchanting landscapes and cultural treasures. Each destination offers a new perspective on the country's rich heritage and natural splendor, making every excursion worthwhile.

Budapest is a city that captures the heart and imagination. Its blend of history, culture, and natural beauty ensures that every visit is filled with discovery and wonder. We hope that this travel guide has provided you with the insights and inspiration needed to fully immerse yourself in the magic of Budapest. May your memories of this remarkable city be as enduring and vibrant as the Danube that flows through it.

We wish you safe travels and unforgettable experiences. Szia és jó utat! (Goodbye and safe journey!)

Thank you for choosing **Tailored Travel Guides***!*

Discover Your Journey

EXTRA RESOURCES

Budapest maps

Budapest General Map

Budapest City Center Map

Buda Transport Map

Pest Transport Map

Budapest Boat Transport Map

Budapest and Surroundings

Budapest Liszt Airport

Budapest Public Transport

Budapest Tourism Office

Budapest City Pass

Hungary's Official Tourist Website

Budapest Keleti Railway Station

Official Taxi Service

City Services

Hospital

TRAVEL

PLACES TO SEE:

LOCAL FOOD TO TRY:

DAY 1

DAY 2

DAY 3

DAY 4

DAY 5

DAY 6

NOTES

PLANNER

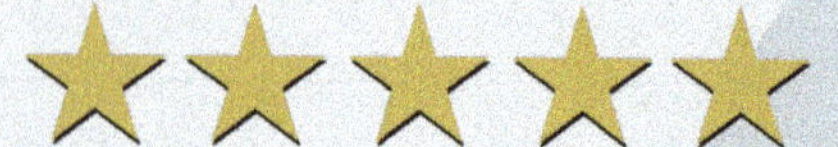

Loved Your Journey With Our Guide? 🌟
Your feedback makes a world of difference! If
our guide helped you explore or enjoy your
destination, we would be thrilled if you could take
a moment to leave us a 5-star review on our
product page.🙏

Simply click the link or go to any of our product
pages on your preferred retailer website and **share
your recommendations.**
https://www.amazon.com/stores/Tailored-Travel-
Guides/author/B0C4TV5TZX

**Scan the QR Code to share your
recommendations**

**Join our Tailored Travel Guides
Network** for more benefits by
accessing this link:
https://mailchi.mp/d151cba349e8/tt
gnetwork
Or by scanning the QR code

Thank you for chosing Tailored Travel Guides!

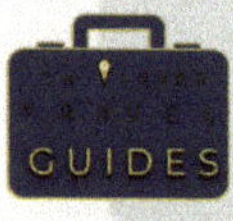

Discover Your Journey

UNLOCK A WORLD OF UNFORGETTABLE EXPERIENCES WITH TAILORED TRAVEL GUIDES!

As your go-to source for personalized and meticulously crafted travel guides, we ensure that every adventure is uniquely yours. Our team of dedicated travel experts and local insiders design each guide with your preferences, interests, and travel style in mind, providing you with the ultimate customized travel experience.

Embark on your next journey with confidence, knowing that Tailored Travel Guides has got you covered. To explore more **exceptional destinations** and discover a treasure trove of additional guides, visit www.tailoredtravelguides.com. or our collection available
on:

Amazon at this link: www.amazon.com/stores/Tailored-Travel-Guides/author/B0C4TV5TZX on **Apple Books**: https://books.apple.com/us/author/tailored-travel-guides/id1741630653?see-all=books
on **Google Play**, at this link: https://play.google.com/store/books/author?id=Tailored+Travel+Guides
on **Etsy**, at this link: https://tailoredtravelguides.etsy.com

Google	Etsy	Apple Books	Amazon

Happy travels, and here's to a lifetime of remarkable memories!

ITALY UNCOVERED SERIES

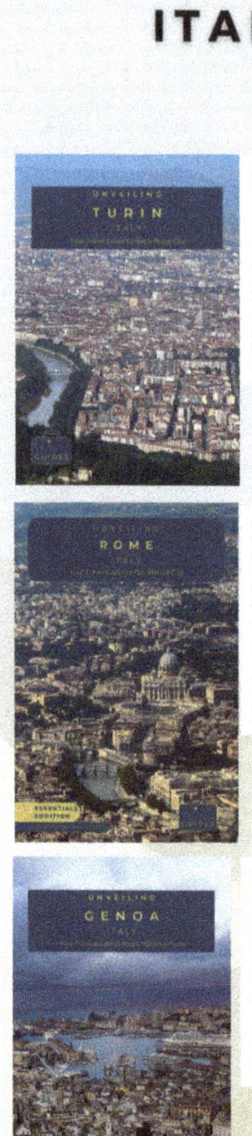
Turin

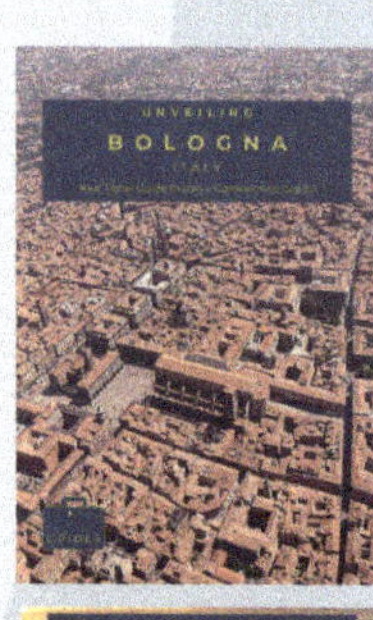
Bologna

Rome

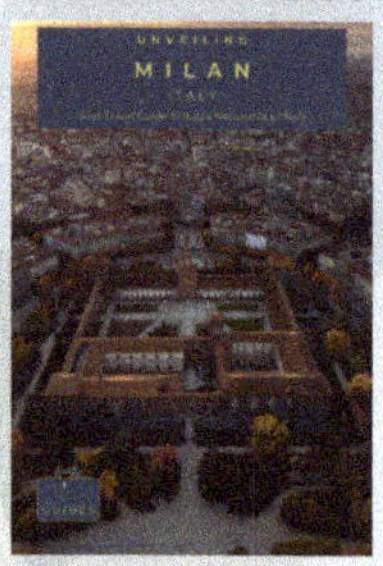
Milan

Genoa

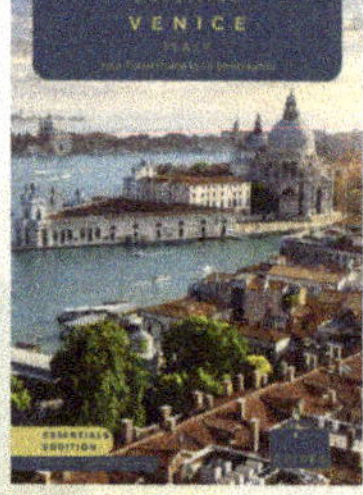
Venice

Verona

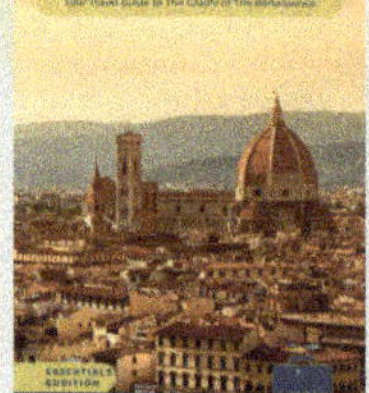
Florence

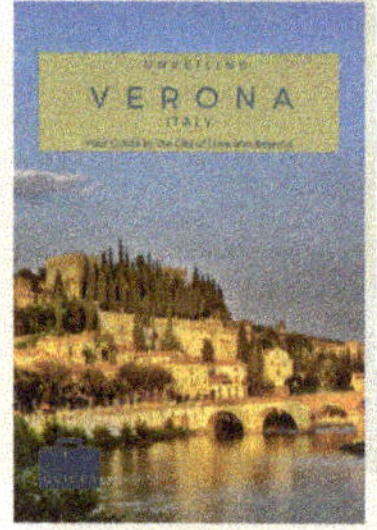
Naples

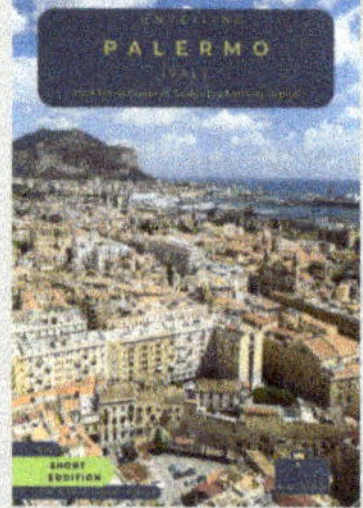
Palermo

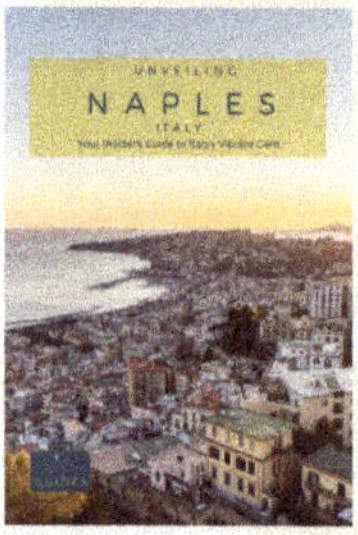

CHECK OUT THE SPAIN UNVEILED SERIES

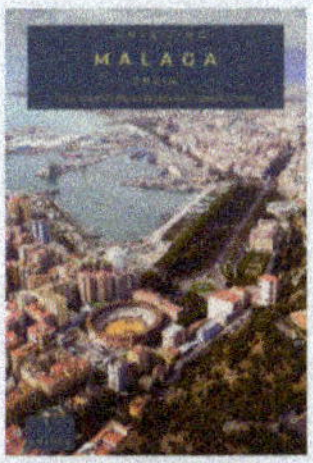

Malaga

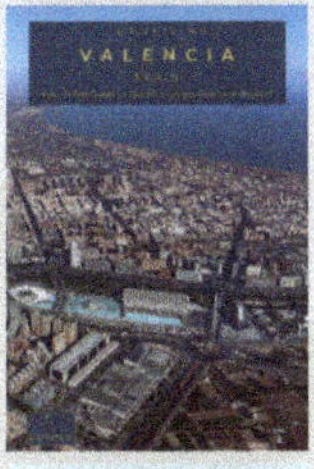

Valencia

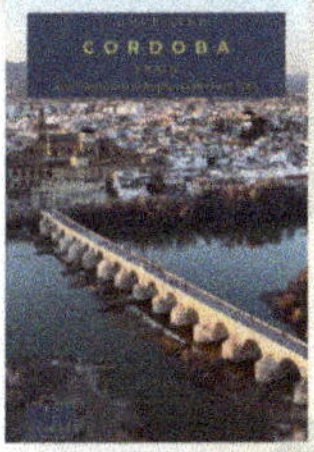

Cordoba

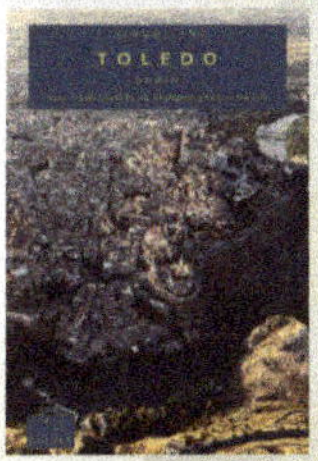

Toledo

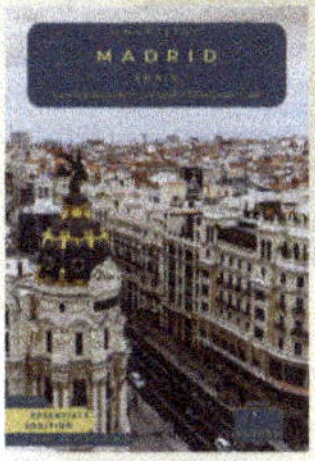

Madrid

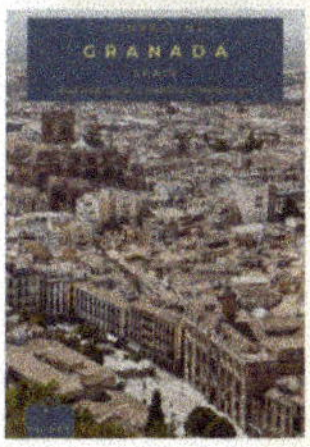

Granada

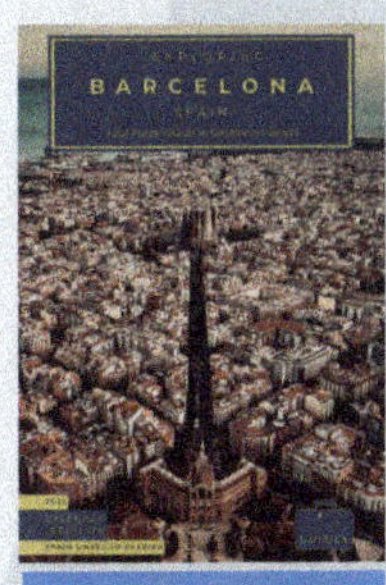

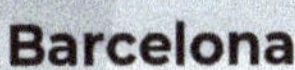

Barcelona

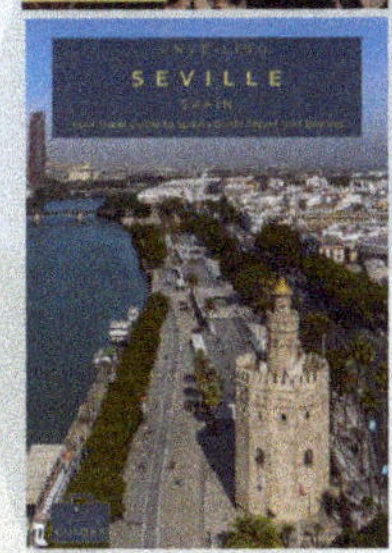

Seville

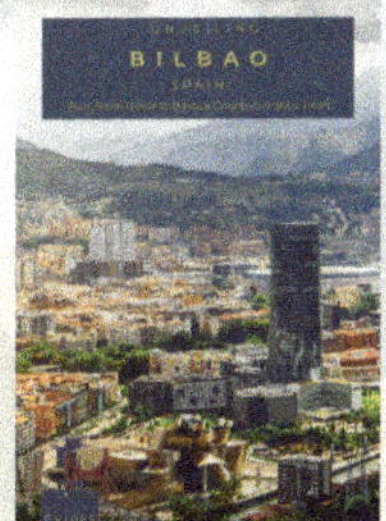

Bilbao

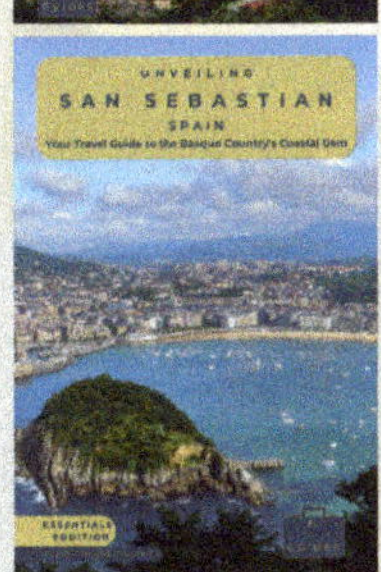

San Sebastian

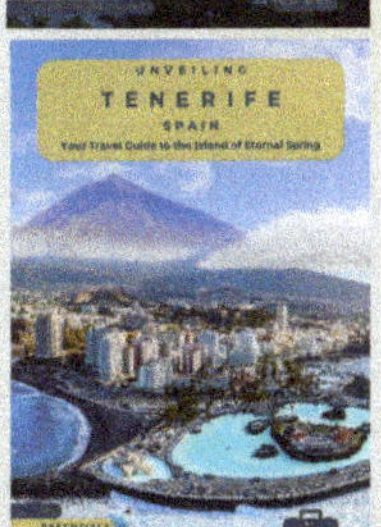

Tenerife

CHECK OUT THE FRANCE UNVEILED SERIES

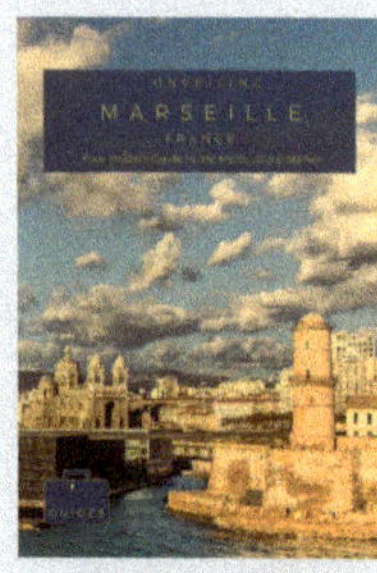

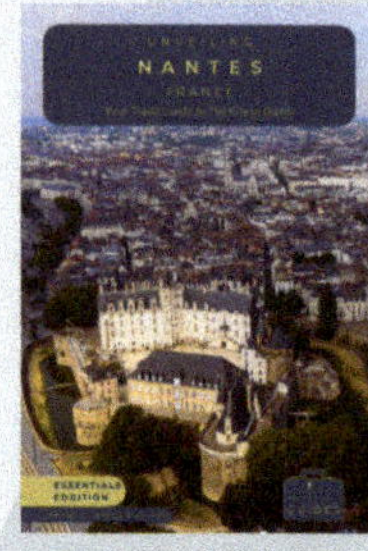

Marseille

Nantes

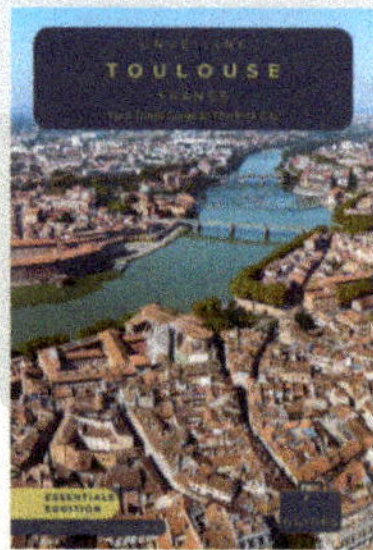

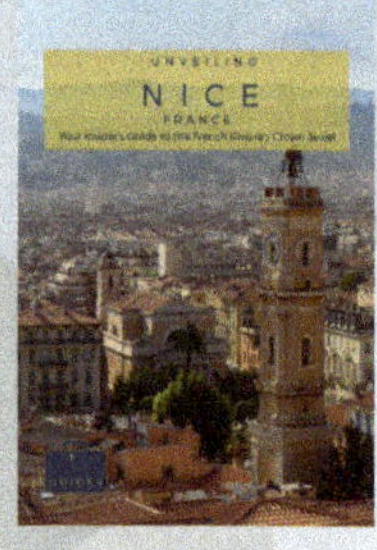

Toulouse

Nice

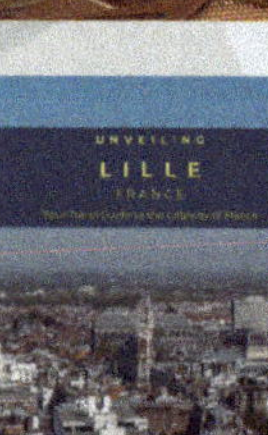

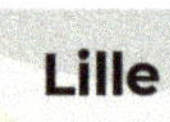

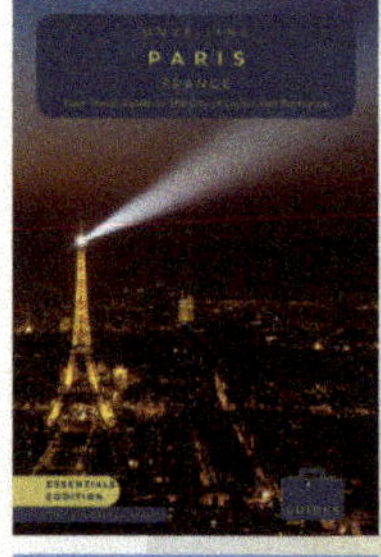

Paris

Lille

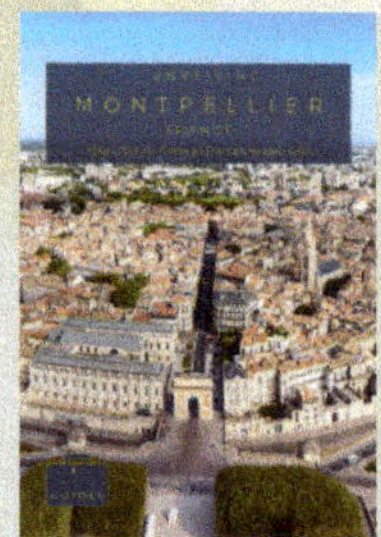

Lyon

Montpellier

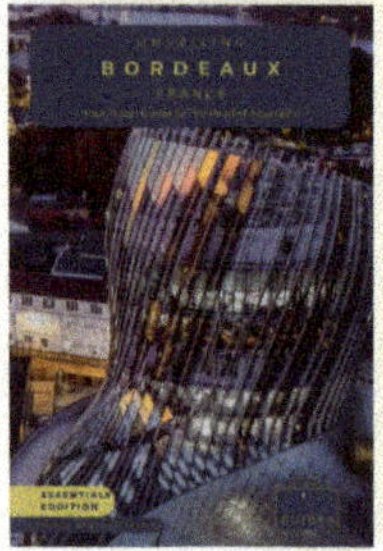

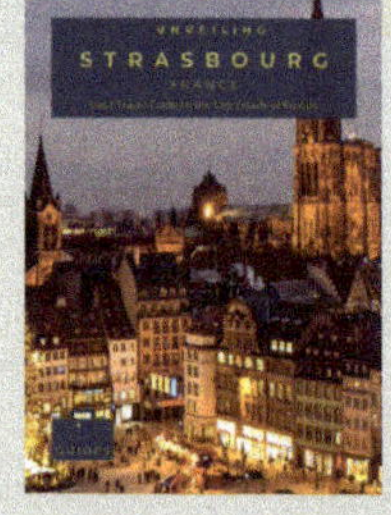

Bordeaux

Strasbourg